MW01596228

A SIMPLER TIME
9 SHORT COMEDIES SET IN OTHER ERAS

by Jonathan Dorf, Tyler Dwiggins, Claire Epstein,
Kathryn Funkhouser, Patrick Greene,
Mora V. Harris, Carrie McCrossen,
Ian McWethy, & Don Zolidis

Playscripts Inc.

Table of Contents

Introduction

The modern age is full of chaos. History is full of important facts and serious hats. We thought, surely a dignified collection of plays set in a simpler time would be instructive for society today! So we waved farewell to a brave band of nine playwrights as they climbed into the secondhand time machine we bought them on the internet. Their mission? To search history and gather the wisdom of the ages into one grand collection of ten-minute plays.

Maybe the time machine wasn't exactly up to code. Maybe we meddled with laws of the universe beyond our control. Maybe history is full of people, and people are ridiculous. All we know is that the plays that came back through the wormhole were historical—but there was something . . . *wrong*.

"Great Scott!" We shouted. "They're humorous! Every last one!"

"BWA HA HA HA," cackled the playwrights, who were either driven mad by the time travel or trying to remind us what comedy is.

If you're reading this, it's already too late. Nine talented playwrights have found the human nature in history and unleashed it upon the world in an unstoppably silly collection.

Some notes on performing the plays:

• This collection is designed to be flexible. Each play can be licensed separately. You may also license the whole collection and only perform the plays that you choose.

• The collection Prologue and Epilogue are short scenes that you have the option of using if you'd like to create a through-line for your evening.

• Each play also has a short, optional Prologue and Epilogue that you have the option of using to thread together whichever plays you've chosen to perform.

• Be sure to properly credit the playwrights and the titles of the individual plays in your programs.

• If you need to make any changes (such as changing a character's gender, or certain minimal language changes), please don't hesitate to get in touch with us. We are happy to run any requests by our authors for their consideration.

If you have any feedback, we'd love to hear from you! We'll listen even if you're not wearing a serious hat.

—The Playscripts Team

7

NOTES ON THE PROLOGUE, EPILOGUE, AND INTERLUDES

Cast of Characters

MARLEY, a genius self-taught scientist who gets stressed out by basic life tasks.

TAYLOR, a laid-back goofball who assumes things will work out, so she doesn't always plan ahead.

CHRIS, a big-hearted idealist who tends towards the dramatic and gets overwhelmed by current events.

Casting Notes

All three characters can be any gender. The script uses female pronouns throughout for consistency, but feel free to modify them to fit your cast.

Production Notes

The characters note that Marley's time machine looks unimpressive, so it can be as simple as a cardboard box or some chairs covered in aluminum foil. A more pathetic vehicle might even be funnier.

You can choose to place the time machine off to the side from your main stage area. In this case, it never has to move and the three characters can join the audience in watching the plays. Or, if your time machine can be easily carried (like a cardboard cutout) or rolled on and off (maybe they're rolling chairs?) you might have the characters exit during the plays and reenter for the interludes.

In the transition into each play, when a "time jump" is indicated, this can be as simple as the trio leaning back in unison going "whoa!" or include other effects—whatever you want, as long as it's consistent each time so it's clear when the transitions end and the next play begins. Maybe your ensemble members can create a low-tech "wormhole" effect by swirling some glow sticks aroud, or swoop by with a sign saying the year where the trio is traveling. These transition scenes can be a fun cover for the scene changes between plays and a chance for your ensemble to get creative. Have fun!

A Simpler Time: Prologue

MARLEY. Thanks for coming over. I wanted to tell you in person, because . . . Well, if I'm right, it's pretty big news.

CHRIS. NO. I'm sorry, but no.

MARLEY. I . . . didn't say what it was yet.

CHRIS. Doesn't matter. I can't deal with any more news. About anything. Ever again. I just can't take it.

TAYLOR. Uh, you've only been paying attention to current events for like a week.

CHRIS. And it broke me! Do you know how much news there is in a week?

MARLEY. Here's the thing, though: *my* news is going to take care of that problem.

CHRIS. News IS problems! Have you seen the news? Turns out, it's NOT GREAT!

TAYLOR. Welcome to being aware of things, my friend.

CHRIS. I thought I would maybe feel better if I dug a bunker in my backyard, but then I found out from the news that the company that makes shovels is actually polluting where poor people live for tax reasons. So now I'm trying to dig my bunker with a stick, and honestly it's going very slowly and EVERYTHING IS TERRIFYING!!!!

TAYLOR. You went from zero to bunker very quickly. Does anybody want to order a pizza?

MARLEY. Guys, listen to me!

CHRIS. I wish a pizza could solve what's happening in the world, Taylor. But it can't.

MARLEY. But I can—

TAYLOR. Look, if it stresses you out, just don't pay attention. Everything will work out.

CHRIS. I can't just stop caring what happens to people. I wish I could go back to a simpler time when pizza could solve all your problems. In elementary school, a pizza party was the greatest possible prize you could achieve. But that's not what life is like anymore. That's not what we have here in the modern world—

MARLEY. —WHICH IS WHY I BUILT A TIME MACHINE.

    (Beat.)

TAYLOR. Sorry, what?

MARLEY. I uh, I built a time machine? So we could return to a simpler time?

TAYLOR. *(Affectionately:)* You would.

CHRIS. You did this just now?

TAYLOR. I thought you were busy, you were going to email that guy back about the big project that you want to do.

MARLEY. I know, I was just kind of procrastinating? You know, you go down a rabbit hole. You send a fun gif of a teeny-tiny horse. Then you look up "can mini horses live indoors," and then you dive into the early career of Jeff Goldblum, and then you teach yourself a lot about nuclear physics.

CHRIS. You do?

MARLEY. Well, long story short, I think I've cracked the space-time continuum, and I've built a time machine.

> *(Beat.)*

TAYLOR. You procrastinated emailing someone back for so long that you invented time travel.

MARLEY. Yeah, do you guys want to go somewhere?

TAYLOR. This is incredible.

MARLEY. I know, I've transcended the laws of space and time!

TAYLOR. No, I mean we can go back to elementary school and get pizza for free!

CHRIS. Taylor, think about this.

TAYLOR. Okay, fine. We can kill Hitler first and then do my thing.

CHRIS. No, I mean. Sometimes they'd order Papa John's. You really think that's as good as it gets?

MARLEY. No no no. *Simpler* time, guys, we're trying to *avoid* things getting complicated. In literally every movie, you change one thing in history and you can mess up the whole future. So we can go wherever we want but we can't change anything.

CHRIS. Hmm, I was hoping we could fix all . . . this. You know, the state of the world.

MARLEY. No, but we can find a time where it was easier to be a person and none of this stuff existed. Take a nice vacation from the horrors of modern life.

TAYLOR. And conveniently, you get an excuse to keep procrastinating and taking a risk on your project.

MARLEY. What? No. Like. Definitely not. It's about, uh, science, and—

TAYLOR. Uh-huh.

MARLEY. Oh, okay. Would a person who's making an excuse make THIS?

(MARLEY *reveals the very unimpressive-looking time machine.*)

TAYLOR. Yes. Yes they would.

CHRIS. Don't take this the wrong way, but that just looks like a cardboard box. (Or *"three rolling chairs" or "a block covered in aluminum foil." Sub in whatever your time machine looks like.*)

MARLEY. Exactly. A lot of people are going to want this technology, so I disguised it to look deceptively low-budget in case it falls into the wrong hands.

TAYLOR. Sure you did.

MARLEY. Get in, I'll prove it to you!

TAYLOR. Okay, so assuming this machine doesn't explode the second you turn it on, where do we go first?

MARLEY. I've been thinking about that. If modern day is the most complicated it's ever been, what could be simpler than the Dark Ages?

CHRIS. Ooh, medieval times! I feel like there was a clear-cut moral code then. Don't you miss chivalry? I miss chivalry.

TAYLOR. I don't remember chivalry because, like you, I was not alive in medieval England.

MARLEY. But I see what you're saying. In medieval times you either have the crown, or you don't have the crown. You're on a quest, you finish your quest. There's none of the gray area. Also I want to know if there's dragons.

TAYLOR. Okay, okay. Let's find out if medieval times were a simpler time.

CHRIS. Hey, you tested that this thing was safe for people, right?

MARLEY. *(Pulling a lever or pressing a button to start the machine:)* I mean I guess we'll find ouuuuuuut.

(Time jump!)

MEDIEVAL MEDICINE
by Claire Epstein

Cast of Characters

FENDREL

WINIFRED

DR. CORNWALLIS

ADELAIDE

Setting

Medieval England.

MEDIEVAL MEDICINE
by Claire Epstein

(Lights up on a sitting room in a small manor house in medieval England. Not a castle, but not a hovel, either.)

(WINIFRED [30s, terribly understanding] sits sewing by the fire. Her husband FENDREL [30s, a blowhard] enters.)

FENDREL. That girl!

WINIFRED. What has she done this time?

FENDREL. She still refuses to marry Lord Cartwright. Some nonsense about how he's one or two decades older than her.

WINIFRED. And he does smell a bit.

FENDREL. Bah! That's just the open trenches of human waste that surround his castle. He's got dozens of servants! What else is he supposed to do with the stuff?

WINIFRED. That is a good point.

FENDREL. How are we ever supposed to move up in the world if our daughter won't marry a lord? Being a merchant is wonderful and everything, but . . . well, it sounds silly to say out loud.

WINIFRED. Tell me.

FENDREL. I want . . . I want . . . to be able to order a beheading. I'm not saying I *would* order a beheading if I were a lord, I'm just saying I'd like the option.

WINIFRED. It's only reasonable. Oh, my poor Adelaide. I wonder what could be the matter with her.

FENDREL. I'm beginning to think that this isn't everyday female hysteria. I think there might really be something wrong.

WINIFRED. Don't say it.

FENDREL. She's a witch.

WINIFRED. No, my dear! She's not a witch. Though I do think she needs help. I certainly didn't put up a fight like this when my parents promised me to you, even though you're so . . . wonderful.

FENDREL. Precisely!

WINIFRED. That's why I've called for a doctor.

FENDREL. So he can diagnose her as a witch.

15

WINIFRED. No, this is one of those new-fangled doctors. Lots of modern ideas.

FENDREL. Bah! "Modern ideas." Back in my day, we'd call a woman a witch and be done with it!

(DR. CORNWALLIS *enters carrying a medical bag.*)

WINIFRED. Ah, here's Dr. Cornwallis now. Thank you so much for coming to see us, and on such short notice.

DR. CORNWALLIS. Of course. Where's the young woman in question?

FENDREL. Adelaide, get in here!

DR. CORNWALLIS. Now, I must warn you that some of my methods may seem strange to you, but I assure you that these are the latest scientific innovations. What are the young lady's symptoms?

(ADELAIDE *enters. She is kind of a pill.*)

ADELAIDE. Whaddaya want now?

FENDREL. There! You hear that? Symptom one: poor attitude.

DR. CORNWALLIS. Mm. And Adelaide, if I were to ask you how your day was going, you would say . . . ?

ADELAIDE. None of your business.

DR. CORNWALLIS. Very interesting. Anything else?

FENDREL. Yes! Symptom two: disobedience.

WINIFRED. She's not terribly interested in the match her father has set up for her, even though the man is a lord and very wealthy.

ADELAIDE. You're so greedy.

FENDREL. Symptom three: casting spells!

ADELAIDE. That wasn't a spell, it was an insult.

DR. CORNWALLIS. I see. Well, I have a few options for you.

(He *takes out a bottle.*)

The first thing that we have to do is get what we men of science call the "bad blood" out.

FENDREL. I'm with you . . .

DR. CORNWALLIS. And the way to do that, is leeches.

ADELAIDE. Leeches! Like we have in the pond?

DR. CORNWALLIS. Don't be ridiculous! These are specially trained leeches.

FENDREL. Don't question the doctor, Adelaide. Symptom four: too many questions. You were saying?

DR. CORNWALLIS. Now, my leeches specialize. For example, Edmund specializes in rashes.

FENDREL. Oo, I could use a session with him.

WINIFRED. What?

FENDREL. Nothing, nothing.

DR. CORNWALLIS. Tristan specializes in gout. Benedict specializes in problems of the mind, and John does everything else.

WINIFRED. And how quickly do they work?

FENDREL. We need something fast-acting. I can't take another moment with this one.

 (He gestures to ADELAIDE.*)*

DR. CORNWALLIS. Fast-acting, you say? Well, there have been some recent studies that bloodletting works more quickly than leeches.

WINIFRED. Studies? That sounds very scientific.

DR. CORNWALLIS. Oh, indeed. A colleague of mine performed bloodletting on at least a dozen wounded soldiers.

ADELAIDE. Wounded? So they were already losing blood?

FENDREL. Hush, child!

WINIFRED. The important thing is that the bloodletting saved the soldiers' lives.

DR. CORNWALLIS. Oh, no. They all died. But they were going to die anyway.

WINIFRED. The important thing is that they felt better as they died from their wounds and the bloodletting.

DR. CORNWALLIS. No, no, they only died from their wounds.

WINIFRED. The important thing is they felt better as they died from their wounds.

FENDREL. Let's do the bloodletting, then. Adelaide, change into something you don't mind getting drenched in blood.

DR. CORNWALLIS. I should warn you about the side effects of bloodletting: dizziness, extreme loss of blood, and death.

FENDREL. All this scientific talk . . . I don't understand it. Now, do you provide the knife, or do I?

ADELAIDE. Wait! There must be other options.

DR. CORNWALLIS. True, but they are a bit riskier.

(He takes a vial out of his bag.)

This is what is called mercury.

FENDREL. Oooo . . .

(He moves to touch the vial.)

DR. CORNWALLIS. No, don't touch it! It's very dangerous.

WINIFRED. Be careful, my dear.

FENDREL. So then how do you use it?

DR. CORNWALLIS. You drink it.

ADELAIDE. I thought you said not to touch it.

DR. CORNWALLIS. Yes, but drinking is fine. And if you experience any difficulty walking, seeing, or speaking, then we can just remove some blood and even everything out again.

WINIFRED. With the leeches?

DR. CORNWALLIS. No, it's the strangest thing. The leeches die if they suck the blood of someone who's had mercury.

FENDREL. Mercury it is! Down the hatch, Adelaide.

ADELAIDE. Please, there must be some other remedy.

FENDREL. More of symptom two, disobedience!

DR. CORNWALLIS. There is one more option. It's called trephining.

WINIFRED. Oh, how scientific.

DR. CORNWALLIS. Yes. It involves drilling a small hole in the patient's head.

ADELAIDE. What?!

FENDREL. I like it already!

WINIFRED. How large would this hole be, Doctor?

DR. CORNWALLIS. It depends on how large the evil spirit is that's living inside your daughter's head.

(He goes over to inspect ADELAIDE's head.)

DR. CORNWALLIS. Now, we could drill the hole here, or here, here might be good, doesn't really matter. Or maybe it does. And then the evil spirit leaves the girl's head, and she's back to normal.

ADELAIDE. And then you plug up the hole?

DR. CORNWALLIS. I'm a doctor, not a miracle worker!

WINIFRED. It does sound rather extreme. We'd need to know that it would really work.

DR. CORNWALLIS. Oh, it's one hundred percent effective. The patient becomes extremely docile, though you do have to be all right with drooling.

WINIFRED. Fendrel drools most of the time anyway, and he's never been trephined. Trephinated?

FENDREL. It's true. Adelaide, sit down and let the doctor drill a hole in your head.

ADELAIDE. Wait! This is insane. There's nothing wrong with me. I just don't want to marry Lord Cartwright because he's old and gross.

(She steps to center stage and pours her heart out.)

It's not that I even expect to marry for love. I know that as a daughter of a merchant, my options are somewhat limited. All I can reasonably hope for is to feel content, and safe, and maybe even happy now and then. Is that so much to ask for?

FENDREL. Witch!

DR. CORNWALLIS. Lord Cartwright, you say? I have an appointment with him next week for bloodletting.

ADELAIDE. Really?

DR. CORNWALLIS. Yes, he said he's courting a young woman and wants to look his best. Wants me to take out as much blood as possible. I didn't know he meant you.

ADELAIDE. Indeed. What time are you to see him?

DR. CORNWALLIS. Midday.

ADELAIDE. I've made a decision. I shall marry Lord Cartwright. Just before the doctor's visit.

WINIFRED. But why the change of heart, my dear?

FENDREL. I know! She was worried her husband wouldn't be healthy enough, and now that she knows the doctor will be visiting, her concerns have been put to rest.

ADELAIDE. That's it. And if the first round of bloodletting doesn't do the trick, you must come back until you've taken all of my husband's blood.

(DR. CORNWALLIS *laughs.*)

DR. CORNWALLIS. All! But then he'd be dead and you would be a wealthy widow.

ADELAIDE. Oh, how foolish of me!

WINIFRED. My daughter is cured!

DR. CORNWALLIS. Are you sure you wouldn't like some trephining? Or a little leeching, on the house?

ADELAIDE. I'm good, thank you.

FENDREL. Free!? I'll take one of those leeches.

DR. CORNWALLIS. Excellent. Just roll up your sleeve. And remember, if you get dizzy, that means it's working.

(*Blackout.*)

End of Play

Interlude 1

Medieval Medicine Epilogue

CHRIS. Okay, so I guess it was still pretty complicated to be a person back then.

MARLEY. I didn't see any dragons at all.

CHRIS. Who cares, we just traveled through time! That's amazing!

TAYLOR. So, was that the simple society you were looking for? You have the crown, you don't have the crown? There's leeches, there's no leeches?

CHRIS. Whatever, it would be lame if we picked the first place we looked anyway. We can go wherever we want.

MARLEY. Yeah, seems like the machine works pretty well. So that's cool.

TAYLOR. "That's cool?" Marley, you've invented the most sophisticated technology the world has ever seen.

MARLEY. I know, right?

Safe Salem Prologue

MARLEY. Okay. Where to next?

CHRIS. I want the simplicity of a small town. Family values! Cows!

MARLEY. Cows?

CHRIS. You said dragons! At least mine's real! I mean, churning butter and stuff. You know your neighbors. Not like now. That sounds simple, right?

TAYLOR. That sounds boring. We have cows now!

MARLEY. I like the idea of everyone knowing each other— No internet, no email. A lot more face-to-face and a lot less anonymous judging.

TAYLOR. A lot more boring. And nobody's going to judge you, Marley. Just email the guy!

MARLEY. It's not about that!

CHRIS. Seems like it is, a little bit.

MARLEY. It's my time machine, I'm making an executive decision! We're going to search for a simpler time in . . . I don't know, 1692.

(Time jump!)

SAFE SALEM
by Jonathan Dorf

Cast of Characters

ABIGAIL WILLIAMS, a teenage Puritan girl.

EMILY WEBB, Abigail's rival, and her age.

JOSEPH CRIBB, a teenage Puritan paperboy wannabe.

MARY PROCTOR, Emily's toadie.

SARAH TWO-SHOES, Emily's other toadie.

JUDGE, a puppet.

GOODY TWO-SHOES, Sarah's mother and a puppet.

BIG TUBA, a sock puppet—different from the other puppets.

THE TOWNSFOLK, puppets.

Setting

Salem, Massachusetts. 1692.

Casting Notes

For a larger cast, feel free to use more puppets (and puppeteers), as the number of Townsfolk is effectively unlimited.

The division of labor with the puppets is up to you, but my recommendation, which allows for two puppets per puppeteer (with the exception of the more involved Judge character), is this:

Puppeteer #1: Judge
Puppeteer #2: Goody Two-Shoes and one of the Townsfolk.
Puppeteer #3: Big Tuba and one of the Townsfolk.

Additional Puppeteers as desired, with each Puppeteer controlling two Townsfolk.

The puppets can be of the Muppet/*Avenue Q* variety, but it's also great (and might be even funnier) if they look totally homemade and cheap (e. g. popsicle sticks). The important thing is to have fun with them! Big Tuba, however, should be the only sock puppet.

Acknowledgments

Special thanks to Reilly Anspaugh, Lucy Keith, Victoria Hallebo, Miya Kodama, Claire Blackwelder and above all to Daniel Rashid, who organized it, for participating in a developmental reading of the play.

SAFE SALEM
by Jonathan Dorf

(Salem, Massachusetts. 1692. A teenage girl, ABIGAIL WILLIAMS, enters. Dressed in Puritan attire, she sweeps the stage for a moment before acknowledging the existence of the audience.)

ABIGAIL. This here is our town. This is our main street.

(Pointing:)

This is our church,

(Pointing:)

and our grammar school—for the boys.

(Beat.)

There's the blacksmith, the cobbler and the tanner. Those are our stocks, and they also double as a platform for hangings and a fire-safe pit for burnings.

(Beat.)

It's a beautiful town, though most people are too busy praying or working to notice.

(Beat.)

It is February 2, 1692. There are no groundhogs here, for we are not German. We are Puritans. Welcome to Salem, Massachusetts Bay Colony.

(Beat.)

You may wonder why I am not saying thee or thou or ye. Wonder no more. Really—stop wondering.

(Beat.)

Our story begins when Abigail Williams, sent on an errand by her father, rushes into the town square.

(No one comes out. Silence.)

ABIGAIL. *(Looking around:)* In a *rush.*

(Beat.)

Oh. This is embarrassing. *I'm* Abigail Williams.

(She pulls out a pair of knitting needles and perhaps some portion of a sweater.)

ABIGAIL. She is behind on knitting a sweater for her youngest brother, John Junior, so she's multi-tasking.

(Enter EMILY WEBB, *also in her teens, reading.)*

EMILY. Enter Emily W—

ABIGAIL. You don't get to say that.

EMILY. You got to—

ABIGAIL. That's because I'm the stage manager.

EMILY. I don't know what that is, but it doesn't sound godly.

ABIGAIL. If everything you didn't know was ungodly, nothing would be left.

EMILY. Mocking is ungodly.

ABIGAIL. Enter Emily Webb.

EMILY. Grrr . . .

(Beat. They walk toward each other. ABIGAIL *has her head down, knitting. They collide.)*

EMILY. Ouch.

ABIGAIL. Now what?

EMILY. You just ran into me.

ABIGAIL. I did?

EMILY. Yes!

ABIGAIL. If I did, I barely touched you.

EMILY. This is so like you.

ABIGAIL. I don't understand why you're getting so upset.

EMILY. Little Miss Perfect.

ABIGAIL. Truly, Emily, I am far too humble ever to brag about my knitting prowess, or how I finished the entire New England Primer before even any of the boys at the grammar school or how people all over the village ask for me rather than their own flesh and blood when their children need minding.

(Beat.)

I know—after I finish knitting John Junior's sweater, I'll knit you a shawl.

EMILY. Grrr . . .

ABIGAIL. You must stop with these animal noises, Emily. People might say they are unholy.

EMILY. *(Exiting:)* Grrr . . . !

(EMILY *is gone.* ABIGAIL *goes back to smiling.*)

ABIGAIL. It's a sleepy little town, where people live simple lives of quiet desperation.

(Enter JOSEPH CRIBB, *teens.)*

ABIGAIL. Good morning, Joseph.

JOSEPH. Good morning, Abigail.

ABIGAIL. It's a beautiful morning.

JOSEPH. Though my knee feels like rain.

ABIGAIL. That's a very useful knee.

ABIGAIL. *(Narrating as* JOSEPH *mimes distributing newspapers:)* Joseph was all set to carry the news from Boston, *Publick Occurrences Both Forreign and Domestick,* but there was only one issue—in September 1690. Still, he walks the route once a month so that he doesn't forget it—in case the paper comes back someday.

(MARY PROCTOR *and* SARAH TWO-SHOES, *also teens, burst onstage.)*

MARY. Help!

SARAH. Help us!

JOSEPH. What's wrong?

MARY. It's— I can't say it.

SARAH. It's— I can't say it either.

(Beat. Somebody's going to need to say something.)

MARY. *(Sotto to* SARAH:) I forgot what we were supposed to say.

SARAH. *(Sotto to* MARY:) Wait—I think I remember.

(Louder:)

It's Emily.

ABIGAIL. Emily . . . ?

MARY. Webb, of course.

SARAH. How many other Emilies are there?

ABIGAIL. Emily Baker, Emily Brand, Emily Lamb.

MARY. Oh.

ABIGAIL. And Emilies Bugby, Bulgar, Chase, Chadwick, Hawke, Irons, Mills, Pickering, Pond, Pynchon and Reynolds.

JOSEPH. There's an Emily Mills?

ABIGAIL. She was just born three days ago.

JOSEPH. If we had a newspaper, we'd know these things.

ABIGAIL. Agreed.

    (Enter EMILY. *She looks exactly as before.)*

EMILY. *(To* SARAH *and* MARY:*)* What's taking so long?!

    (To ABIGAIL:*)*

You!

ABIGAIL. What's wrong?

EMILY. Can't you see?!

JOSEPH. Is that a smudge on your frock?

ABIGAIL. That will come right out with a little water.

EMILY. My eyeball. You stole my eyeball!

ABIGAIL. Your eyeball is right where it's always been. And so is the other one. Right, Joseph?

JOSEPH. Uh . . . I do see two eyeballs.

EMILY. That's because she's bewitched me so that people see my eyeball—where it is not.

SARAH. Yes.

MARY. We see it too. It must be so.

ABIGAIL. Why would I steal your eyeball? I have two perfectly good eyeballs.

EMILY. Just like you have three perfectly good younger siblings to mind at home, but no, you have to mind everyone else's.

ABIGAIL. What?

EMILY. What? Stop looking at me like I just had an inner monologue.

    (Getting back on track:)

Sarah, what did we learn in church about eyeballs?

SARAH. That witches steal eyeballs for the Devil, and in return he grants them the power to fly and float.

EMILY. *(To* SARAH, MARY *and* JOSEPH:*)* When she bumped me, that's when she did it. She floated my eyeball right out.

MARY. I think I saw it.

SARAH. Yes, we thought it was the fluttering of a tiny, gentle hummingbird, but I'll bet it was your eyeball.

EMILY. See? Witnesses. Witch!

ABIGAIL. Wait—

MARY. Help, witch!

ABIGAIL. Stop!

SARAH. Quick, Mary—cover your eyeballs so she can't steal them.

(MARY *and* SARAH *cover their eyes with their hands.*)

ABIGAIL. I'm not a—

SARAH. Witch!

ABIGAIL. Joseph, tell them—

JOSEPH. Abigail, you've always been really nice —

EMILY, SARAH, and MARY. Witch!

ABIGAIL. Joseph, tell them it's not true.

JOSEPH. I think—

EMILY, SARAH, and MARY. Witch!

ABIGAIL. Joseph, tell—

JOSEPH. *(Exiting in a hurry:)* I think I better go over my paper route again. It could come back any day.

(*And he's gone. Enter* TOWNSFOLK, *including a* JUDGE. *They are all puppets. Feel free to give them pitchforks and torches. Among the townsfolk are* BIG TUBA, *the only sock puppet, and* GOODY TWOSHOES, *who is* SARAH's *mother.*)

TOWNSFOLK. Where's the witch?
Where are the witnesses?
Where's the judge?
Trial!

ABIGAIL. This is all a big misunderstanding—

EMILY. Abigail Williams has always been a little too perfect, and now we know why. She steals eyeballs, and . . .

MARY. And . . .

(*Coughs:*)

Makes us choke.

SARAH. Yes, lots of choking.

(SARAH *coughs.*)

ABIGAIL. Now you're just being ridiculous.

SARAH. And she, uh . . .

MARY. Yes, she . . .

EMILY. She charms babies.

ABIGAIL. Well, babies do love me.

EMILY. But not in a good way.

JUDGE. Abigail Williams, I sentence you to—

ABIGAIL. Wait!

JUDGE. What?

ABIGAIL. Don't I at least get a trial?

TOWNSFOLK. Yes, give the witch a trial.
Trial first, then the sentence.
Let us not be hasty, friends.
As long as we're quick about it.
Witch!
String up the witch!

JUDGE. Order! We will have order here!

(*To* ABIGAIL:)

My apologies, child. I was so consumed by my lust for justice I forgot.

(*To the others:*)

Trial by water!

TOWNSFOLK. Dunk the witch!
Throw her in the lake!
Get the rocks!
Heavy rocks!
Lots of heavy rocks!

ABIGAIL. Wait!

JUDGE. If you're not a witch, you have nothing to fear. Your body may sink, but your soul will go straight to heaven.

ABIGAIL. No—wait!

JUDGE. Now what?

ABIGAIL. Whatever I may have done, it is only because I am possessed by the spirit of . . .

JUDGE. Of . . . ?

ABIGAIL. *(To the Audience:)* I'm not proud.

> *(Back in the scene:)*

Big Tuba!

BIG TUBA. You did not just call out the sock.

TOWNSFOLK. She looks like the devil's instrument to me.

BIG TUBA. I'm a sock.

JUDGE. Big Tuba—

TOWNSFOLK. I always wondered how you pronounced that.

ABIGAIL. And . . . I am also possessed by the spirits of Emilies Baker, Brand, Lamb, Emilies Bugby, Bulgar, Chase, Chadwick, Hawke, Irons, Mills, Pickering, Pond, Pynchon and Reynolds. And Emily Webb.

> *(There's a collective gasp from the* TOWNSFOLK.*)*

EMILY. That's ridiculous. You stole my eyeball. If anything, you're possessing me.

SARAH. You said Emily Mills is three days old.

ABIGAIL. Easy pickings for witches like Emily Webb . . . and Mary Proctor and Sarah Two-Shoes . . .

JUDGE. Goody Two-Shoes, is your daughter a witch?

GOODY TWO-SHOES. *(Coming forward:)* She's not a— Wait—there was that one time our butter was sour . . .

SARAH. Mother, that wasn't—

TOWNSFOLK. Throw her in!
Throw them all in!
Trials for all!
Why are we wasting the rocks?
We know they're guilty!
Hang them all!

JUDGE. Citizens of Salem, we need to be calm.

TOWNSFOLK. Hang the witches!

JUDGE. Order! We will have order!

ABIGAIL. Your honor, as you can see, I am an innocent victim here.

EMILY. I'm the victim.

SARAH and MARY. We're the victims!

JUDGE. Quiet! The most important thing is that Salem remain safe from witches.

TOWNSFOLK. Safety first!
Zero tolerance for witches!
Leave no stone unturned!
Practice safe Salem!

JUDGE. And the only way to know that for sure is for all of us to go to the lake.

> *(Beat.)*

I'll go in last in case any witches bob to the surface.

> *(Beat.)*

TOWNSFOLK.	**EMILY.**
To the lake!	Wait—I was kidding about the eyeball.
TOWNSFOLK.	**ABIGAIL.**
Get the rocks!	And about the Emilies!
TOWNSFOLK.	**EMILY, ABIGAIL, MARY, & SARAH.**
Save our town!	And everything!

> *(They all exit amid sounds of a mob. Beat. All grows quiet. Enter JOSEPH. He looks around.)*

JOSEPH. Hello?

> *(Beat.)*

Where did everyone go?

> *(Beat.)*

I guess I'm the stage manager now. I wish I knew what that was.

> *(Beat.)*

Uh . . . it's gotten dark over Salem. You can still see a few candles in windows, and a few stars. And a bunch of gurgling sounds from the lake. I reckon it's close to midnight. Time to get some rest—in case there's a newspaper to deliver tomorrow. You get a good rest too. Goodnight.

End of Play

Interlude 2

Safe Salem Epilogue

TAYLOR. I gotta say, small towns are a lot less boring than I thought.

CHRIS. You know, I wanted to go back in time to *avoid* angry mobs.

MARLEY. Well, the judging wasn't anonymous. It was face-to-face. I'm not sure if that's . . . better. Especially if you're a sock.

TAYLOR. *(Philosophically:)* Probably tough to be the only sock in town in most times in history.

CHRIS. Probably tough to be the only *anything*. Because of the mobs.

MARLEY. Yikes. Didn't really think about *that* whole aspect.

TAYLOR. Hey, I just want to say that if we lived back then, I wouldn't accuse you guys of witchcraft. Even if I got jealous of you.

CHRIS. I would have to be *really* mad at you.

MARLEY. Wow. Okay. I see how it is.

Founding Fathers (Mothers) Prologue

TAYLOR. I think we should find you some inspiration to take a risk on that project of yours.

MARLEY. Ugh, I already invented time travel today, though.

CHRIS. Yeah, you're a genius. That's why it's so ridiculous.

TAYLOR. Let's go to a collaboration on something that worked out well for pretty much everybody. Mostly . . . Well, for some people.

MARLEY. Ooh, we're going back to when Destiny's Child formed?

TAYLOR. I was thinking when the Founding Fathers wrote the Constitution.

MARLEY. You're right, I might get overwhelmed when faced with the potential in a young Beyoncé.

TAYLOR. But if you do want inspiration to start a band instead, I am still open to letting you guys be in my band.

CHRIS. Again, none of us sing or play instruments, including you.

MARLEY. Let's go see those founding fathers.

TAYLOR. So that's a "maybe" on starting the band?

MARLEY. Absolutely not.

    (Time jump!)

FOUNDING FATHERS (MOTHERS)
by Don Zolidis

Cast of Characters

TOM

ALEX

JAMES

DOLLY

ELIZA

MARTHA

Setting

The night before the Constitution is due. 1787.

FOUNDING FATHERS (MOTHERS)
by Don Zolidis

(Late at night. ALEX and JAMES are seated at a table, tearing their hair out over a draft of the Constitution. TOM is pacing, paper in hand.)

TOM. All right, read what we've got so far.

(Hands a piece of paper to ALEX.)

ALEX. It's the same as when I read it last time.

TOM. I want to hear it again.

ALEX. You're perfectly capable of reading it yourself.

TOM. Just read it, Alex.

JAMES. Guys. Chill. We're not getting anywhere. Let me read it.

TOM. Fine.

JAMES. "We the people, in order to form a more perfect union . . ."

ALEX. How can something be more perfect? It's either perfect or it's not. What the heck.

TOM. Dude.

JAMES. Come on, man.

ALEX. It makes no sense. More perfect? "Hey that thing is perfect. You know what would make it more perfect? Nothing! Nothing can make anything more perfect!" That's the whole point of the word "perfect"!

JAMES. It's just a word. Chill.

ALEX. Let's look up the definition of the word perfect.

(TOM walks away from the table.)

TOM. I can't work like this! IT'S DUE TOMORROW.

ALEX. Yeah, and I wasn't the one who decided to wait until the night before to work on this project.

JAMES. Can we work on this now? Can we focus for five seconds? Please?

ALEX. Fine.

JAMES. I never shoulda picked you for my group.

ALEX. That's hurtful.

TOM. All right, what else do we have?

JAMES. What are you talking about? That's all we have.

TOM. We've got eleven words?

ALEX. One of which is redundant.

JAMES. How is this a surprise to you? You two have just been fighting this entire time.

TOM. I thought you were writing stuff down while we were talking!

JAMES. I was doodling. See? Here's a picture of a monster with big teeth.

ALEX. Why were you drawing a picture of a monster?!

JAMES. It's eating Jefferson.

ALEX. Ha!

JAMES. You're the bones under its feet.

ALEX. How can we have a Constitution if you're just drawing pictures of monsters?!

JAMES. Cause you idiots won't stop fighting!

TOM. Fine! We'll stop! Let's focus. Think of something good everybody. Put the draft in front of us and let's all stare at it AND NOT SAY ANYTHING for five seconds.

(They all stare at the paper.)

(Pause.)

ALEX. "More perfect" is stupid.

(TOM and JAMES groan in pain and walk away from the table.)

What?! It is! You want something stupid in the FIRST SENTENCE?!

JAMES. WE DON'T EVEN HAVE A SENTENCE WE HAVE TWO CLAUSES!

TOM. I swear, when I write my autobiography, I am trashing you two dudes.

ALEX. Perfect. Oh wait, no, more perfect!

TOM. MORE PERFECT IS ACCEPTABLE!

ALEX. TO ALIENS MAYBE!

JAMES. DUDES. COME ON. STOP.

TOM. I—can't—work—with—him.

ALEX. You're not working at all, so it's not a problem.

JAMES. Can I remind you guys that this is due tomorrow? If we show up with nothing, the whole Constitutional Convention is gonna go with the stupid New Jersey plan.

TOM. Even the name of it is terrible: New Jersey plan. I hate those guys.

ALEX. Word.

JAMES. All right so let's quit fighting over stupid stuff—we will table the "more perfect" issue for the moment and move on to the next clause, all right? Okay? Can we do that?

ALEX. Fine.

TOM. Thank you.

JAMES. We the people . . . in order to form a . . . union . . . do . . . hereby?

TOM. Yes.

JAMES. Ordain.

TOM. How about establish?

JAMES. Compromise. Ordain and Establish.

ALEX. THEY'RE THE SAME WORD.

TOM. SHUT UP!!!

ALEX. THEY MEAN THE SAME THING. Look it up! Here is a dictionary!

JAMES. Kill me. Someone kill me.

ALEX. *(Reading:)* "Ordain: To cause something to exist." "Establish: To create something." THEY'RE THE SAME THING. ARE WE GETTING PAID BY THE WORD HERE?

JAMES. I can't work like this. I can't.

TOM. This is why you're gonna die in a duel someday.

ALEX. I'll duel right now. I got my pistols outside.

JAMES. Can you please stop?

ALEX. I can't help it if I have standards and Tom just wants to put whatever in there. Like, "oh hey let's have a garbage document to found the country, nobody's gonna read this thing anyway."

TOM. It doesn't have to be perfect.

ALEX. Maybe we should make it more perfect!

JAMES. All right look—you two donkeys shut your mouths for a second—let me go check on the girls and see how they're doing.

ALEX. Fine.

(*Lights up on a different part of the stage.*)

(DOLLY, ELIZA, *and* MARTHA *are sitting together working on their own version.*)

ELIZA. Oh that's nice, Dolly.

MARTHA. I like that.

DOLLY. So I'm thinking that we have this whole amendment process where people can change things if we need to. That way, the document can change over time.

MARTHA. That is so brilliant.

DOLLY. Thank you, Martha. And I've been loving your ideas too.

MARTHA. That means so much to me.

ELIZA. I think that we need to make sure there's a series of checks and balances; that way the presidency won't get too powerful. Cause there's gonna be, like, male presidents for a long time. And they're pretty irrational.

MARTHA. It's the hormones. Drives them nuts. "Oh I gotta go fight something cause I'm stupid." It's exhausting.

ELIZA. Don't get me started on Alex.

DOLLY. I hear that. James has got short man syndrome super bad.

ELIZA. So let's say the Congress passes laws, and the President signs the laws, and the Supreme Court judges whether or not they're constitutional.

MARTHA. Sounds good.

DOLLY. Let's make sure Congress has the responsibility to declare war. Cause you know how guys are.

ELIZA. Right? "Stop looking at my country like that. You wanna fight?!"

MARTHA. The worst.

ELIZA. It's every day with Alex. "My honor is being impinged! Here's my ten rules of dueling!"

MARTHA. He's so extra.

ELIZA. You know he literally carries a pocket dictionary with him just to look up words to argue about?

MARTHA. Guys, can we focus on finishing the Constitution please? I know the boys are hormonal. We don't have to talk about it.

ELIZA. It's a good thing we started working on this last week.

MARTHA. Before we keep going—I wrote these thank-you notes to you guys.

(MARTHA *hands out notes.*)

For being amazing partners.

DOLLY. Oh my gosh that is so thoughtful. And you know what? I made zingers for us.

(ELIZA *waves her hands in front of her face to ward off tears.*)

ELIZA. Ah! You guys are the best. I love us.

(JAMES *enters cautiously, followed by* ALEX *and* TOM.)

JAMES. Hey.

ELIZA. Hey.

ALEX. Hey.

DOLLY. Hey.

JAMES. So um . . . how's your version coming?

DOLLY. Basically done.

JAMES. Sweet.

ELIZA. How are you guys doing?

JAMES. Um . . . we're pretty much done too.

ALEX. It's practically perfect. It could probably be more perfect, I guess.

TOM. So um . . . We need something to turn in tomorrow—and it would probably be best if we like combined our groups—just to help you.

JAMES. Definitely. So people don't laugh at your ideas. Cause, you know, you're girls. Nobody takes you seriously.

ELIZA. Thanks for the reminder.

(ALEX *takes up their draft and starts looking at it.*)

ALEX. I mean there's probably a lot of problems in here—so we'll just fix them. You guys can go home. No worries. There's probably some girl stuff you have to attend to.

JAMES. Cleaning and whatnot.

TOM. Which is super important—cause we respect you.

MARTHA. I just want to be clear—we want to make sure our names are on it.

ELIZA. Yeah we did a lot of work on this.

TOM. Absolutely.

ELIZA. We totally want credit. And fifty bucks.

ALEX. What?!

MARTHA. You guys didn't do any work.

TOM. We're writing the preamble, which is the most hardest part.

ELIZA. Oh please. Fifty bucks. Now.

    (The guys get some money out of their pockets.)

TOM. All right, all right fine.

    (He hands over some money.)

DOLLY. *(To* TOM:*)* You just put your face on this and wrote "two dollars."

MARTHA. *(To* ALEX:*)* And you just put your face on this one and wrote ten.

TOM. Why is yours worth five times as much as mine?

ALEX. Cause I'm five times better.

JAMES. Well that's all we got.

MARTHA. Fine. Here you go.

    (The boys take the draft and exit.)

DOLLY. That was nice.

ELIZA. Well I'm charging double for the amendments.

DOLLY. Hey do you think we should have specified that women get the right to vote?

MARTHA. No I mean that's obvious, right?

    (Lights down.)

End of Play

Interlude 3

Founding Fathers (Mothers) Epilogue

MARLEY. So I think what I learned is that procrastination usually works out well for people.

CHRIS. Well CERTAIN people.

TAYLOR. That wasn't the lesson!

MARLEY. I'm pretty sure that was the lesson.

CHRIS. I thought it was that the past is sexist! And also that someone always does all the work in group projects!

MARLEY. That too.

Lady Washington Prologue

CHRIS. Okay, I've had enough of being depressed about America. Let's get inspired. I want to go back to when politics were simple and noble and true.

MARLEY. You don't get enough of politics now?

CHRIS. I guess I just mean, when politics brought us together instead of driving us apart. When an election was like, "let us create a soaring eagle of democracy together" instead of everyone yelling at each other for two years on the news. Because the first priority is the country. The first priority is the stars and stripes. The first priority is . . . freedom.

TAYLOR. You sound like a Fourth of July car commercial.

MARLEY. Do you want to go salute George Washington or something? Would that make you feel better?

CHRIS. Yes I do. When America was new and nothing was divided. A simpler time.

MARLEY. Are you running for something?

CHRIS. I don't know! Maybe I should!

  (MARLEY *initiates the time jump.)*

TAYLOR. Maybe you shouuuuuulllllllllddd . . .

  (Time jump!)

LADY WASHINGTON
by Tyler Dwiggins

Cast of Characters

GEORGE

MARTHA

ADVISOR

ANNOUNCER #1

ANNOUNCER #2

REFEREE

COACH #1

COACH #2 (non-speaking)

ELIZA HAMILTON

Setting

1789, George and Martha Washington's house

Casting Notes

ANNOUNCER #2 and ELIZA can be doubled.
ADVISOR and COACH #2 can be doubled.

LADY WASHINGTON
by Tyler Dwiggins

(*Lights up on* MARTHA *and* GEORGE WASHINGTON *in the bedroom of their beautiful home.* GEORGE *holds up two suit jackets, one red, one blue.*)

GEORGE. I don't know, is red too obvious? I want something that says, "I'm a capable leader" but also "I'm relatable." But still . . . intimidating? No, not intimidating. Imposing.

MARTHA. Can a jacket say all that?

GEORGE. It has to! But it needs to be slimming too

MARTHA. You're putting a lot of pressure on this, dear.

GEORGE. So you think go with the blue?

MARTHA. (*Beat.*) Sure.

GEORGE. Think about it, Martha. Other people will follow in my footsteps and . . .

MARTHA. And you want them to wear the same jacket as you?

GEORGE. Sort of! (*Beat.*) Do you know what you're wearing?

MARTHA. To the . . . ?

GEORGE. Yeah, to the . . . You have something ready, don't you?

MARTHA. Yeah, I have something ready.

GEORGE. Well let's see it then? What are you wearing to the Inauguration?

(MARTHA *can't meet his gaze.*)

MARTHA. Well . . . About that . . .

GEORGE. Yes?

MARTHA. You remember that time I went to Ben Franklin's surprise party by myself, because you didn't want to?

GEORGE. Yes.

MARTHA. And I wanted to make sure nobody was offended by your lack of attendance, so I told everyone you had explosive diarrhea?

GEORGE. You really didn't have to do that.

MARTHA. I had to say something!

GEORGE. You could have just said I was "sick" or better yet, "busy."

MARTHA. People like to be told a specific lie. They don't take it as personally. They feel like you put some work into rejecting them.

GEORGE. Why are you bringing this up?

MARTHA. Because I need you to make up an excuse for my absence. I'm not going to the Inauguration, George.

GEORGE. You what?

MARTHA. I'm not going?

GEORGE. What do you mean you're not going?

MARTHA. It means when everyone's there, I'll be somewhere else. I'll be absent. Not present. Away. Predisposed. Unavailable—

GEORGE. I get that! Where in God's name will you be?

MARTHA. That's up to you. You can make something up.

GEORGE. You're not coming on MY big day?

MARTHA. I'm not.

GEORGE. Why are you doing this to me? What will people think when I show up alone? I'm going look like such a fool!

MARTHA. Listen, George, I don't want to embarrass you, but I don't approve of this . . . job title.

GEORGE. You mean the President of the United States? You don't like that sound of that?

MARTHA. I don't. Why are we elevating ourselves above other people? Like we're better than them? We're no more equipped to rule over people than the King we just left behind.

GEORGE. Not rule. Govern.

MARTHA. Potato, potahto. Power corrupts.

GEORGE. But it'll be me. And I'm really delightful. *(Beat.)* Right?

(MARTHA *can see that* GEORGE *is feeling very insecure.)*

MARTHA. You are delightful, dear. The most delightful. But we came all this way, started a revolution so that all people could have an equal voice. I believed in that, and I thought you did too.

GEORGE. C'mon, Martha.

MARTHA. We just got through a war together. Wouldn't you like to relax for a while?

GEORGE. It's my responsibility to guide this country.

MARTHA. It's also your responsibility to pick up your socks and you ignore that one!

GEORGE. Martha, this could be a real opportunity for both of us. Think of the power you'll hold!

MARTHA. What kind of power is that?

GEORGE. I don't know! We could figure it out together. Nobody's done this before. America is an experiment!

(MARTHA *hadn't thought of it this way. She considers.*)

MARTHA. What would I be called?

GEORGE. Called?

MARTHA. My title. You're President. I'm what?

GEORGE. Hmm. I hadn't thought of that . . . Presidentess?

MARTHA. Meh.

GEORGE. Miss America?

MARTHA. *(Higher-pitched:)* Meh.

GEORGE. First Lady?

MARTHA. *(Highest pitched:)* Meh.

GEORGE. What's wrong with that?

MARTHA. It sounds like you've got more than one lady.

GEORGE. Be serious, Martha.

MARTHA. I am! It sounds like you've got a whole harem.

GEORGE. Can't you just show up to support me? Even if you don't support the job itself, can't you support that I'll be the one doing it?

(MARTHA *considers it.*)

MARTHA. I can't do it, George. I'm sorry if that hurts you, but I feel it in my bones, this is the wrong direction for this country. I love you, and I will return when this hoopla ends. But I won't be there to bless this union.

(MARTHA *exits, just as an* ADVISOR *enters behind* GEORGE *unnoticed.*)

ADVISOR. WHAT?!

(GEORGE *jolts, startled.*)

GEORGE. Oh my, you scared me.

ADVISOR. You should be scared! How's it going to look if your own wife doesn't show up?

GEORGE. Not great.

ADVISOR. Nobody's going to think you can run a country if you can't even run your own household. George, there's only one way to settle this . . . A duel.

GEORGE. *(Solemnly:)* I know.

(A loud, anachronistic song blares. Something frenetic like "Turn Down for What." MARTHA re-enters. MARTHA and GEORGE begin doing exaggerated athletic stretching. A CROWD gathers and the space transforms into a boxing ring.)

(An ANNOUNCER introduces the opponents. GEORGE flexes and preens.)

ANNOUNCER #1. In one corner we've got Mr. President himself! He's a fearless general and our new commander in chief! His teeth are wooden, but his heart is gold! Geoooooorrrrrge Waaaaaaaashingtoooooon!

(The CROWD screams and applauds! We hear them scream things like: "Go George go!" "Crush her!" and "I'll marry you!")

ANNOUNCER #2. And in his opponent, we have a woman who needs no introduction! She's got powder in her wig and fire in her eyes! Maaaaaaarthaaaaa Waaaaaaashingtoooooon!

(MARTHA flexes her biceps and then does a formal curtsy. The CROWD screams and applauds! We hear shout of "YAS MARTHA!" "SLAY, QUEEN!" "WERK, MARTHA!" A stern REFEREE steps up to MARTHA and GEORGE.)

REFEREE. Now I want a good clean fight between you two, you understand me? You two know the rules?

GEORGE. Yes, sir.

REFEREE. Alright then, get in fighting stance.

(The REFEREE brings out some sort of podium. It can be an ornate marble post or just a simple bar stool. MARTHA and GEORGE crouch down and put get into position for their battle; a thumb war. They clasp their hands together and hold their thumbs aloft, with fiery glances in their eyes.)

MARTHA. 1, 2, 3, 4! I DECLARE A THUMB WAR

GEORGE. 5, 6, 7, 8! COME TO MY INAUGURA . . . tion

MARTHA. *(Disappointed:)* Oh George.

GEORGE. You know, Martha, there's still time to back out of this. We don't need to make a spectacle of ourselves.

MARTHA. I was going to say the same thing to you.

ANNOUNCER #2. Now, we've never seen a thumb war quite like this between a public official and his wife. This is quite unprecedented isn't it?

ANNOUNCER #1. It is. But every couple finds their own way to settle disputes. My wife recently signed a declaration of independence from me!

ANNOUNCER #2. *(Laughs:)* Oh Chuck, you're such a kidder!

ANNOUNCER #1. *(Still laughing:)* I'm not! My wife moved out last week!

ANNOUNCER #2. Oh. Sorry to hear that, Chuck.

(We hear the "ding ding ding" of the bell.)

REFEREE. LET'S GET READY TO THUMBLE!!!

(MARTHA and GEORGE begin to thumb wrestle.)

ANNOUNCER #2. Now that's interesting, we're seeing Mr. Washington take strong offensive strides. He is really going after her.

ANNOUNCER #1. That's correct. Mrs. Washington seems to be on the defense.

MARTHA. George, I don't want to embarrass you . . . But I will.

GEORGE. Hardly! This is for my country!!!

(The CROWD roars. GEORGE makes a gain. He presses MARTHA's thumb down. The REFEREE swoops in for a closer look.)

REFEREE. One! Two! THREE!

MARTHA. Noooo!

(A bell dings.)

ANNOUNCER #2. That's the end of a very short first round and Mr. Washington already has the lead.

ANNOUNCER #1. But it's not over 'til it's over! We still have two rounds to go.

(MARTHA runs over to her COACH.)

MARTHA. I'm so sorry, coach.

COACH. Don't be sorry. Just be better. You've got two more rounds.

> (*The* COACH *holds out a bottle of Gatorade, which* MARTHA *drinks through a straw. She runs back over to the podium. She and* GEORGE *return to their battle positions. We hear the dinging of a bell and Round #2 begins.* MARTHA *squirms her thumb out from under* GEORGE's.)

GEORGE. You know, you can't win this, Martha. I won the Revolutionary War, what have you ever won? A quilting bee?

MARTHA. How dare you, George? EVERYONE is a winner in a quilting bee!

> (MARTHA *smashes her thumb on top of* GEORGE's.)

REFEREE. One! Two! THREE!

> (*The bell rings. A disgusted* GEORGE *wiggles his thumb out of* MARTHA's *grip.*)

GEORGE. Who do you think you are?

> (*He storms over to his* COACH, *who wipes* GEORGE's *face with a towel.* MARTHA *slumps down in a stool in her corner of the ring. Her* COACH *throws a towel over her shoulders.*)

MARTHA. I don't know if I can keep this up.

COACH. You have to, Martha. You started this, now finish it.

MARTHA. But how??

COACH. Let him do the work. Tire him out.

> (MARTHA *nods. "Eye of the Tiger" blares as she gets into fighting position and the thumb war continues. The lights flash in and out to indicate the passage of time as the thumb war wages.* GEORGE *is going crazy, bouncing back and forth, moving his thumb in assorted wild patterns.* MARTHA *holds back.*)

> (*The* CROWD *goes from wildly excited to polite golf claps to clear boredom. Some of the audience is sleeping.*)

ANNOUNCER #2. This has to be some kind of record! We're at nearly three hours.

> (GEORGE *wipes sweat from his face with his free hand. He is tiring out.*)

MARTHA. You're looking tired, dear.

GEORGE. (*Panting:*) I . . . don't . . . get . . . tired.

MARTHA. You seem so . . . worn out.

GEORGE. *(Panting:)* I . . . will not . . . be deterred.

(GEORGE's *thumb is cramping.*)

GEORGE. Oh my god! No!

ANNOUNCER #1. It can't be?

ANNOUNCER #2. After all this?

ANNOUNCER #1. A thumb cramp?!

(MARTHA *smashes her thumb down onto* GEORGE. *The* CROWD *erupts!*)

ANNOUNCER #2. We have our victor! Martha Washington won the thumb war and will not be attending the inauguration!

(*The* CROWD *exits, chattering about the duel.*)

MARTHA. Are you okay, George?

GEORGE. I am . . .

MARTHA. Are you . . . mad?

GEORGE. You won fair and square . . . America is a place where we are free to disagree. I'll miss you at the Inauguration though.

MARTHA. I'll see you at home.

(MARTHA *kisses him on the cheek.*)

(*The lights fade and we transition to the Inauguration. Very formal, patriotic music plays in the background. The* CROWD *are now guests of the ceremony.* ELIZA HAMILTON *enters.*)

ELIZA. My dear George, congratulations.

GEORGE. Thank you, Eliza. I appreciate you attending this gathering.

ELIZA. Oh, everyone in New York wants to be at this party. Where is your beautiful wife?

GEORGE. I fear an illness kept her back in Virginia. *(Whispers:)* Explosive diarrhea.

ELIZA. Ah . . . You didn't have to tell me that.

GEORGE. Sorry.

ELIZA. Well, at any rate, I hope you'll save me a dance later tonight?

GEORGE. I will, Mrs. Hamilton.

(GEORGE *walks away to mingle with other guests at the party. With a change in lighting, we hear a hip-hop beat snapped by the party guests, with spare piano chords.* ELIZA *steps into a spotlight.)*

ELIZA. *(Rapping:)* Martha Dandridge Washington / Her name was Martha Dandridge Washington / She had irritable bowel syndrome / but just today, just todayyy

(The ADVISOR *steps in behind her. The music ends.)*

ADVISOR. I'm sorry, could you please stop doing that?

ELIZA. I'm breaking the fourth wall

ADVISOR. We JUST had the fouth wall polished, Eliza!

ELIZA. I just wanted to tell the audience that although this account has been fictional, Martha Washington really did not attend George's inauguration. Some historians believe she was finishing up last-minute affairs in Virginia, but—

ADVISOR. Historians? What are you talking about? That all just happened this week.

ELIZA. *(To the audience:)* You guys can just look it up later.

ADVISOR. Who are you talking to?

(Blackout.)

End of Play

Interlude 4

Lady Washington Epilogue

CHRIS. I can't believe this! Even the very first guy and his own wife couldn't agree?

MARLEY. I guess the good news is, America was never *not* divided.

TAYLOR. That's hilarious.

MARLEY. It's sort of comforting that we were always like this.

CHRIS. Comforting HOW?

MARLEY. They stayed married! And America's still here, so.

CHRIS. For HOW LONG, though?

TAYLOR. We could actually find out.

Selfie Portrait Prologue

TAYLOR. Okay, come on, this is all too educational. I wanna fight some robots. Let's go to the future!

MARLEY. I don't know if this thing does the future . . .

TAYLOR. Oh, as opposed to the extensive safety testing you did to go to the past?

CHRIS. We can't give up on the whole past when there's so much we haven't seen. We've been looking at politics—what about, like, high society instead? Where they're just worried about being polite and civilized and waltzing and stuff.

TAYLOR. I think that's just being rich.

MARLEY. No, I know what you mean. British people just writing each other letters about who they're going to marry.

CHRIS. What fork to use. "Do you have your gloves, madam?"

MARLEY. "Does he have an amiable reputation?"

TAYLOR. What are you even talking about?!

MARLEY. That sounds soothing. That could be a simpler time. The 1800s, maybe? Give me a year.

TAYLOR. You would rather do that than fight robots? Really?!

CHRIS. How about . . . 1821?

MARLEY. Let's go.

(Time jump!)

55

SELFIE PORTRAIT
by Carrie McCrossen

Cast of Characters

AGATHA CHESTERTON WINTHROP

VAN DER CRISP, an artist.

TWIG, a servant.

MARJORIE

YOUNGER ARTIST

Setting

1821, a glorious country estate.

SELFIE PORTRAIT
by Carrie McCrossen

(It's the year 1821. We're in a glorious country estate. On one side of the stage, AGATHA CHESTERTON WINTHROP sits for a portrait. Her pose can be whatever you desire. I hope it's something silly.)

(On the opposite side of the stage, VAN DER CRISP, the preeminent portrait artist of his day, is facing an easel, putting the finishing touches on a portrait.)

(There's no reason we ever need to see the finished artwork, unless you have a particularly eager props department.)

(VAN DER CRISP pauses. Looks. Finishes . . . One. Last. Brush. Stroke. Ahhh.)

VAN DER CRISP. My lady. After countless hours of labor these past three weeks, I am pleased to announce that I am finally finished with your portrait.

(He stands from his easel and stretches. LADY WINTHROP stays seated.)

WINTHROP. *(Without moving her mouth too much:)* Does this mean I can move?

VAN DER CRISP. Yes, my lady. We are finally done! Finally we have a work of art as beautiful as the subject it represents!

WINTHROP. You're too kind, Master Van der Crisp. It has been a pleasure sitting for the world's most gifted and famous portrait artist.

VAN DER CRISP. You flatter me. I humbly shine the mirror up to life.

(LADY WINTHROP rises.)

WINTHROP. Well? May I see it?

VAN DER CRISP. Of course. Voila!

(He picks up the canvas and twists it so that she can see it. [OR . . . he ushers her to his side of the stage to view the canvas on the easel.])

WINTHROP. *(Overjoyed:)* It's—it's—it's me!

VAN DER CRISP. Yes, my lady!

WINTHROP. Why—you've perfectly captured the curls of my hair, the cleft in my chin! It's my likeness absolutely! You truly are as gifted as everyone says.

VAN DER CRISP. Thank you but I'm far too modest to admit that.

>   *(Beat.)*

WINTHROP. My only thought is . . .

>   *(She cocks her head as she stares at the painting.)*

Does it look *too* much like me?

VAN DER CRISP. I'm not sure what you mean, my lady.

WINTHROP. It is accurate, to be sure. It shows all my qualities exactly as they are. But perhaps it is too realistic.

VAN DER CRISP. I am a Dutch master. Realistic is literally what I do.

WINTHROP. Yes of course. But think who will view this portrait! It is not just for me and my family. It will be viewed by all of SOCIAL. (That's what I call society.) It will be seen by my friends in Bruges who are very prone to gossip. It will be viewed by my exes! I must make a positive impression. They must like it.

>   *(Beat.* VAN DER CRISP *stares at her with amazement. No one has ever criticized his work before.)*

VAN DER CRISP. No one has ever criticized my work before.

WINTHROP. It's not a criticism! It's just . . . could we not make some changes? Could we not accentuate my eyes a bit? Or perhaps make my waist a tad smaller than it appears?

VAN DER CRISP. My lady. You ask—

WINTHROP. Please! Please, Master Van der Crisp! Just some minor changes. Perhaps if you painted me from a more flattering angle? TWIG!

>   *(TWIG, a servant, appears.)*

TWIG. Yes, Ma'am.

>   *(Noticing the portrait:)*

Ooh. That's a nice portrait, my lady!

WINTHROP. Oh you like everything, Twig. Fetch the stool.

>   *(TWIG exits and returns immediately with a stool.)*

If you stand up there you'll get a nice angle. I've always thought I looked nicer "Up from Down."

TWIG. Yes Ma'am. Much better than "Down from Up."

(*She poses as before.*)

VAN DER CRISP. My lady—

WINTHROP. Oh do it, I'm paying you.

(VAN DER CRISP *steps awkwardly onto the stool and now must reach downward to touch the easel with his brush.*)

VAN DER CRISP. Yes, my lady. As you wish.

(*—BLACKOUT—*)

(*—LIGHTS UP—*)

(*It's 1821. Same country estate. Three months later.* LADY WINTHROP *and* VAN DER CRISP *are in the same positions we left them. Except now* VAN DER CRISP *has a beard.*)

(VAN DER CRISP *finishes . . . One. Last. Brush. Stroke.*)

VAN DER CRISP. My lady. It has taken three months, but I am pleased to announce that I have finally finished my *second* attempt at your portrait.

(*He stands from his easel and stretches.* LADY WINTHROP *stays seated.*)

WINTHROP. Excellent! May I see it?

VAN DER CRISP. (*This time a little more lackluster:*) Voila.

(*He picks up the canvas and twists it so that she can see it.*)

WINTHROP. Yes exactly. This is what I always envisioned. It's me. But like a *better* version of me. My eyes really pop. My cheekbones— did you highlight them?

VAN DER CRISP. Yes, my lady. I took a page from Caravaggio and got creative with the lighting.

WINTHROP. Very wise! Very wise!

(*Beat. She stares at the painting a little more closely.*)

But do I not look old?

VAN DER CRISP. No. You look perfect. You—

WINTHROP. TWIG!

(TWIG *appears.*)

Do I look old?

TWIG. In real life, ma'am? Or in the painting? To be honest, ma'am, in real life you've seen better days. You have not moved from your position for over four months while you've been posing for Master Van der Clipp's fine painting. In fact, I think you might have some bedsores underneath them dresses—

WINTHROP. I was asking about the painting, Twig!

TWIG. Oh. Apologies, Ma'am. In the painting you look very fetching indeed. Though I suppose Master Van der Pump's keen eyes have spotted a wrinkle or two on your brow.

VAN DER CRISP. It's Van der Crisp—

WINTHROP. Yes! That is what I feared! Master Van der Crisp, you *must* make another attempt. I cannot let the world see a portrait in which I have brow wrinkles—

VAN DER CRISP. But you *do* have brow wrinkles!

WINTHROP. I know! Of course I do! I'm twenty-six! I'm an old married woman. But I cannot have wrinkles *in the portrait.* I've already told you the importance of this. I need to get those likes!

VAN DER CRISP. My lady, I have spent long enough on your portrait. I must travel home and rest. My health is not what it used to—

WINTHROP. Duchess Fanny Bestchester's last portrait got 67 likes— (that's 67 people who said aloud that they liked it) —and it's driving me mad! I simply must get more likes than her!

TWIG. Master Van der Camp makes a good point, my lady. Perhaps you should take a break and spend some time with your family. Your daughter is at such an impressionable age and you haven't seen her in months.

WINTHROP. My daughter! Goodness, I almost forgot about Marjorie. Bring her in, will you, Twig?

>(TWIG *exits and immediately* MARJORIE *runs in, giving her mother a hug.* MARJORIE *is seven.*)

MARJORIE. Mama! Mama! It is so wonderful to see you at last!

>(*Let's pronounce this like the English. With the accent on the second syllable. MaMA.*)

MARJORIE. I have so much to tell you! I rode a horse. And Mister Probst said I have a gift for the piano forte. Oh and a bird made waste on Father's head while we walked to church!

WINTHROP. How marvelous! I want to hear all about it, my darling! But first Mama must sit for another portrait.

MARJORIE. But you've already been sitting for so long!

VAN DER CRISP. *(Angrily:)* Yes. You've already been sitting for so long.

WINTHROP. Nonsense! You must make one more attempt, Van der Crisp. And this time without any wrinkles!

> (MARJORIE *reluctantly slumps off as* LADY WINTHROP *settles back into her pose.*)

> (VAN DER CRISP *reluctantly steps back onto his stool.*)

WINTHROP. Wait! You'll need something to help you avoid the wrinkles. Some kind of flattering lens to . . . FILTER your vision. Let me think . . . filter . . .

> *(She thinks.)*

Of course! My stockings!

> (She slips off her stockings from under her dress. [You could also do this with a scarf.])

VAN DER CRISP. My lady, please don't make me wear your dirty stockings as a blindfold—

WINTHROP. Oh do it. Or I won't recommend you on YELP—

VAN DER CRISP. Ye Olde List of Painters? But you must! That's how everyone finds portrait painters these days!

> *(He wraps the stockings around his eyes like a blindfold.)*

> *(—BLACKOUT—)*

> *(—LIGHTS UP—)*

> (It's 1824. Same positions. VAN DER CRISP's beard is now grey.)

> (VAN DER CRISP finishes . . . One. Last. Brush. Stroke.)

VAN DER CRISP. *(Exhausted:)* And. Done. Voila.

> (He turns the canvas to face LADY WINTHROP. She takes a look at it.)

WINTHROP. I feel like we're getting *closer.*

> (VAN DER CRISP's head might explode.)

WINTHROP. Let's talk lighting. Twig? Can you dim the lights?

> (From offstage, "Twig" dims the lights. VAN DER CRISP groans as he gets back on his stool.)

> *(—BLACKOUT—)*

(−LIGHTS UP− Same estate. Later.)

(VAN DER CRISP paints, exhausted. LADY WINTHROP poses. TWIG enters.)

TWIG. My lady, you asked me to inform you if any more people liked Duchess Bestchester's portrait.

WINTHROP. I did.

TWIG. Well, the chimney sweeps all liked it. So that's seven more.

WINTHROP. Heavens! How can I compete with that? Wait! I know what gets lots of attention . . . Twig, fetch me a puppy. Or kitten! Or baby! Where is Marjorie?

TWIG. Marjorie is grown and moved to America, my lady.

WINTHROP. Oh darn. Well, a kitten then!

(VAN DER CRISP sighs loudly.)

(−BLACKOUT−)

(−LIGHTS UP− Same estate. Later.)

(Now LADY WINTHROP holds a stuffed puppy or kitten. [Or honestly any stuffed animal.])

WINTHROP. Wait. Stop. I need you to start over and this time I'm going to be making this face:

(She makes an intense duckface.)

VAN DER CRISP. My lady. You cannot expect me to paint you with that face. You look like . . . a duck.

WINTHROP. *(Speaking through her duckface:)* A DUCK WITH MORE LIKES THAN LADY BESTCHESTER!

(−BLACKOUT−)

(−LIGHTS UP− Same estate. Later.)

WINTHROP. *(Suddenly:)* KITTY EARS! I need KITTY EARS and a little tongue that sticks out of my mouth!

VAN DER CRISP. That's insane.

WINTHROP. DO IT! WE'RE SO CLOSE!

(−BLACKOUT−BEAT.)

(−LIGHTS UP−)

(Same estate. Year is up to you. LADY WINTHROP's hair is now grey.)

(VAN DER CRISP has been replaced by YOUNGER ARTIST, who is just finishing his/her final brush stroke.)

YOUNGER ARTIST. I'm finished, my lady.

WINTHROP. May I see it?

(He turns the canvas to face her. She slow-claps.)

WINTHROP. Congratulations, Van der Crisp.

YOUNGER ARTIST. Master Van der Crisp died on the job fourteen years ago, my lady. I'm his replacement. My name is Brunch. *(Pronounced "Broonch".)*

WINTHROP. Yes of course. Brunch. Well congratulations. I think you've finally done it.

(The YOUNGER ARTIST *is stunned.)*

YOUNGER ARTIST. Really? You don't think your eyes are "too big" or that you look "thirsty" like you're "trying too hard?" Any of the things you complained about in the past?

WINTHROP. No. Perhaps it is my glaucoma, but this looks perfect to me. I cannot wait to share it with all my friends! TWIG!

(TWIG enters. He is very old.)

WINTHROP. Twig! Invite the ladies from Bruges, invite my exes, invite all my friends from social—even my rival, the much-liked Lady Bestchester!

TWIG. Would that I could, my lady. But all your friends are dead.

WINTHROP. Dear me. And Marjorie?

TWIG. Lives in America with her five children, where she runs a successful cattle farm!

WINTHROP. Glad to hear she's doing well. But what do I do? At last I have this glorious portrait and no one to share it with.

(The YOUNGER ARTIST *starts to pack up his easel to leave.* TWIG *tries to comfort his mistress.)*

TWIG. Perhaps you can just enjoy the portrait yourself, my lady.

WINTHROP. *(Distraught:)* Myself? No. That won't do. The whole point of the portrait was to project something to others. I've worked so hard . . . I've spent my entire life chasing the praise of others.

(Beat. She has a breakthrough.)

What have I done? I've been so focused on how this portrait would appear to others that I've neglected all my friendships and relationships, and now that it's finished I have no one to share it with. This is a real awakening for me! I may be old but I can still change! I can stop caring about the "image" I project to others. I can learn to be myself!

(YOUNGER ARTIST *has made his way to the door . . .*)

YOUNGER ARTIST. Well . . . that's a lofty goal. Best of luck to you, madam. I'll just be leaving—

WINTHROP. Where do you think you're going? No one's going anywhere until we come up with the PERFECT CAPTION!

YOUNGER ARTIST. NOO!

(*Blackout.*)

End of Play

Interlude 5

Selfie Portrait Epilogue

CHRIS. I really thought people with handkerchiefs were better than us.

MARLEY. We're more efficient at being obsessed with ourselves.

TAYLOR. And we don't carry around what we sneezed in our pockets. Handkerchiefs are gross. You know who I bet would not waste a lot of time being obsessed with themselves? Robots.

MARLEY. I'm not trying to be a buzzkill here. I just really don't know what's going to happen if we travel the other way.

Weekend Warriors Prologue

TAYLOR. Well are y'all done romanticizing the past yet?

CHRIS. I like that you're writing off the entire past. Come on, there's plenty of things that were simpler in the past.

MARLEY. What about work. Honest work. With your hands. In the dirt. For an honest day's pay.

TAYLOR. You could have that, if you go back to the present and email that guy!

MARLEY. No I mean like, WORK. Like, real . . . work. With sparks and wheels and . . . sweating.

TAYLOR. If real work is sweating, then me dancing around my house to Robyn is working.

CHRIS. Yeah, it is! Work, girl!

MARLEY. No, no, no. I think it must have been simpler to work in the past. You do one thing all day. You're not trying other stuff you don't know about. Nothing has to change.

TAYLOR. None of this "trying," none of this "facing your fear of rejection."

MARLEY. No, I mean for the sake of debate. Work was better back in . . . give me an era.

CHRIS. Let's do Victorian times. I have to say, your commitment to procrastination is truly impressive.

MARLEY. I'm not procrastinating!

(Time jump!)

WEEKEND WARRIORS
by Kathryn Funkhouser

Cast of Characters

HELEN

DORA

RUBY

MR. GORDON

Setting

The Knickerbocker Shoelace Factory, 1918

Production Note

All we need to see of the factory is a table and some cardboard boxes.

WEEKEND WARRIORS
by Kathryn Funkhouser

(At a work table in the Knickerbocker Amalgamated Shoelace Factory, HELEN, RUBY, and DORA pack shoelaces into boxes. They are all really, really tired. In fact, RUBY has dozed off, head propped up on her hand. HELEN slowly picks up her hand, which is attached to a box.)

HELEN. I think I might be so tired that I glued myself to this box.

DORA. Be careful, Mother . . . . I mean—sorry . . . Helen. Sorry. I'm a little tired too.

HELEN. That's all right. Who doesn't hallucinate on the job now and then? But we're halfway done! Eight hours down, eight to go.

DORA. Please don't have a positive attitude right now, I can't bear it.

HELEN. How are you holding up over there, Ruby?

(RUBY snores.)

DORA. I envy her.

(MR. GORDON enters, a frazzled but well-meaning man with a booming voice, startling everyone and waking RUBY up as he bellows:)

GORDON. Aaaand how are my most industrious little worker bees doing today?

RUBY. *(Jolting awake:)* — Wha?

(HELEN and DORA try to distract him to cover for RUBY.)

HELEN. SHOELACES! Just so many shoelaces we're making to-day . . .

DORA. Another scintillating day here at the factory! Yes sir . . .

HELEN. Shoelaces here! Shoelaces there!

DORA. Just living how I always dreamed!

RUBY. *(Scrambling to look like she wasn't sleeping:)* Very—alert, and productive, and alert. Sir.

(Beat. GORDON sizes up the three of them suspiciously.)

GORDON. *(To HELEN:)* Is that a box glued to your hand?

HELEN. . . . No?

GORDON. Ladies, please. Sales are down here at the Knickerbocker Amalgamated Shoelace Factory. Only eight more hours! We must keep production quick like bunnies who are very afraid of losing their jobs!

RUBY. *(Rubbing her eyes:)* Hop hop hop, Mr. Gordon.

GORDON. Pardon me?

RUBY. *(Through a big yawn:)* Like a baaAAhhunny. Sorry. Like a bunny.

    (HELEN *loses her shoe as she hurries* RUBY *away.)*

HELEN. She's complying with what you said about the bunnies, sir.

DORA. Of course, we try to embody all the animals you compare us to.

GORDON. *(To* HELEN:*)* I think your shoe fell off.

HELEN. Oh sorry, sir. They're my sister's and the shoelace broke the other day.

GORDON. Well that's absurd! You can't represent the Knickerbocker Amalgamated shoelace factory with inferior shoelaces on your own shoes! Why on earth wouldn't you buy some? You know how slow our sales have been! You're the problem that keeps me awake at night! You're the problem with America!

HELEN. . . . Well, I didn't mean to be the problem with America, but I'm working sixteen-hour days for the next twelve days. So I'm not sure when I can get to the store?

DORA. Maybe she could take a break to go buy some.

GORDON. Yes and *I'll* take a break to go to *Paris* where I don't have to listen to people making ridiculous suggestions.

RUBY. Pardon me, Mr. Gordon, there's one thing we *could* try. My brother works for Henry Ford at his factory.

GORDON. Ford? That man with the automobiles?

DORA. Well he had an idea that I thought was really something. You know how everybody works incredibly long days, every day, while barely hanging on to consciousness for most of it?

GORDON. Sure.

RUBY. Well, it turns *out* you actually get *more* work done if the week starts on Monday and ends on Friday, you work eight hours, and you're awake the *whole time.*

HELEN. . . . Wait. You're saying, the week . . . ends?

RUBY. And you don't hallucinate or anything? Wow.

GORDON. Ha! So first this Ford fellow's putting horses out of work so we can ride around in machines, and now he's pulling *people* out of work to go SLEEP? Let's see how THAT works out for him!

DORA. I think it already worked out for him. He's incredibly rich.

HELEN. That seems like it's worth a try.

GORDON. Ah, it's fun to dream isn't it? But this is business, my little songbirds. See you in a couple hours, ladies! If you need a drink of water, you're fired!

RUBY, HELEN, DORA. Thank you, Mr. Gordon.

(*He exits.*)

DORA. If I have to go one more day like this I'm going to burst into flames.

HELEN. We've got to convince Mr. Gordon that it's better for him *and* for us *and* for the shoelace factory if we have a week that ends!

RUBY. Now, keep in mind, I'm incredibly sleep deprived, but I think I have an idea. I have to warn you though . . . it's extreme.

HELEN. I don't know . . .

DORA. What's the idea?

(*RUBY whispers to them.*)

HELEN. That's very extreme.

DORA. I'm sorry, but he's left us no choice.

(*Blackout.*)

(*The next day—* GORDON *enters.*)

GORDON. Aaaaand, good morning, you dear little chipmunks of the forest.

(*The girls stand in unison. It's a little menacing.*)

Ladies . . . what is this?

HELEN. A-five, six, seven, eight!

(*They launch into an impassioned interpretive dance—perhaps something in the vein of "9 to 5" or "Everybody's Working for the Weekend" would serve well? Depending on how much you care to dance, this could either be a full little number or literally be one dramatic pose before* GORDON *cuts it off.*)

GORDON. *(Dangerously quiet:)* How *dare* you. How *dare* you try to convince me to change my labor practices via interpretive dance?

RUBY. We—we just thought, we've seen you dancing in the stairwell when you think nobody's looking, so we thought you might be inspired . . . ?

GORDON. *(Swelling with emotion:)* For your information, my *dream* was to be a dancer on the music hall stage. But when my father found out, he said, "Be a man, Gordon. A man who ensures that the family shoelace factory remains profitable no matter what the human cost, or you're dead to me."

RUBY. My mistake.

GORDON. Helen, you lost your shoe again.

> *(He exits.)*

DORA. All right. So what now?

> *(If you think it would be fun, the music could kick up again under the following. This quick series of short scenes acts like a montage as the workers try a new tactic each day:)*

> *(DORA, RUBY, and HELEN exclaim over a newspaper as GORDON enters and crosses the floor.)*

HELEN. Why, it says here that Henry Ford's the richest man in town!

GORDON. *(Without breaking stride:)* We all know you don't know how to read, Helen.

> *(GORDON exits.)*

> *(The next day. As MR. GORDON enters, they turn around the cardboard boxes—a letter or two is painted on each one so it spells out "WEEKENDS PLEASE.")*

> *(MR. GORDON shakes his head and twirls his finger around. They sheepishly turn the boxes back around and sit down, discouraged, as he exits.)*

> *(The next day. They go fetch even more boxes and pile them up into an impressive pyramid, just as GORDON enters.)*

HELEN. Mr. Gordon, we worked so hard that we doubled our shoelace output in just eight hours.

GORDON. Wonderful!

RUBY. So we can go home?

GORDON. So you can double *that* in the *next* eight hours, my swift little antelopes!

(He exits.)

(Next day. The others quickly pile boxes on RUBY *like they fell on her somehow.)*

DORA. Noooooooooo!

HELEN. Mr. Gordon, Mr. Gordon, come quick!

DORA. Why?!?! Why would destiny cut down a young woman in her prime?!?!

HELEN. Too much.

DORA. Okay.

*(*GORDON *runs in and sizes up the situation.)*

GORDON. Oh boy. What happened? Are the shoelaces okay?

HELEN. It's Ruby! There was an accident!

GORDON. Oh, all right. Well, how are we supposed to make our numbers now?

DORA. She was so exhausted from working so many days in a row she made a fatal mistake.

*(*GORDON *starts picking up the boxes and making sure they're okay, uncovering* RUBY *but taking no notice of her.)*

GORDON. I can't believe I have to find another girl now.

HELEN. You know, maybe if she wasn't so tired . . .

RUBY. *(Dramatically, like a movie death scene:)* So . . . tired. If only I was well-rested, this accident was so . . . preventable.

GORDON. So are you too mangled to work? Helen, can you go down to the orphanage and see what little kids are available?

RUBY. *(Sitting up like she's miraculously springing back to life:)* No, no, I can still do my job! I'm good! Barely!

HELEN. But I think we all learned something.

GORDON. Yes, that women are too clumsy to work in factories.

HELEN. No! That if you let workers rest, they won't die in horrible accidents so much.

DORA. We did have that fellow who was crushed by machinery downstairs.

GORDON. Who, Jim?

DORA. I was thinking of Jake. But, him too.

GORDON. What am I supposed to do, remember the names of the dozens of people who die in horrible accidents here?

HELEN. This factory is incredibly dangerous.

GORDON. Yes, I can't believe you people are so bad at staying awake. But it's all right, my chickadees, the inventory is fine.

DORA. Thank goodness.

GORDON. I know! Let's go ladies! Busy beavers, busy beavers!

    (He exits.)

HELEN. All right, so maybe the answer isn't appealing to his better nature.

RUBY. I have an idea.

DORA. We're not doing interpretive dance again.

RUBY. No. We're going on strike!

    (The next day. DORA, HELEN, *and* RUBY *march around the table. Maybe they have clever signs.)*

DORA, HELEN, & RUBY. What do we want? Weekends!
When do we want them? Saturday and Sunday!
What do we want? Weekends!
When do we want them? Saturday and Sunday!

GORDON. What in the name of Pete are you doing?

DORA. Nothing, Mr. Gordon. Absolutely nothing.

RUBY. We're not going to make a single shoelace until we get some reasonable hours.

GORDON. Don't you understand? I can't indulge these little silly-goose whims of yours! We have shoelaces to sell! I have things to prove to my father!

DORA. You spend an awful lot of time calling us busy beavers and worker bees. So maybe you could use a reminder that you ought to treat us like human beings.

GORDON. I'm RELATING to you. I'm being NICE, you insipid little—

HELEN. — Hey, don't talk to her like that!

GORDON. Compose yourself, Helen. You can't even keep your shoe on.

HELEN. You know what? That's it. That's the last straw! It's so ironic I could explode! I work at a shoelace factory, I make money by making shoelaces, I am literally SURROUNDED BY SHOELACES and all I want is two seconds to buy one for myself! Isn't this supposed to be the American Dream? Don't I work incredibly hard? Don't I come in every day with a positive attitude? I have such a great work ethic that I annoy Dora!

DORA. I resent her! She's right!

HELEN. I'm not asking for the moon, Mr. Gordon. I'm not asking to be treated like a queen! I'm asking for enough time to myself to go buy myself a shoelace, so my shoe stops falling off, so everyone LEAVES ME ALONE.

(*Beat.*)

GORDON. Wait, you're saying, if you had more free time you would . . . buy a shoelace?

HELEN. I dream about it at night.

GORDON. You mean, if I gave you time off, you would use that time to buy shoelaces, thereby boosting the sales of the Knickerbocker Amalgamated Shoelace Factory?

HELEN. I guess so.

GORDON. In that case, Helen . . . I have an incredible idea.

(*Maybe the music from the interpretive dance kicks back in.*)

And it's called . . . ..

(*A flourish of a dance move.*)

. . . the weekend.

HELEN. I'll take it.

(*Blackout.*)

End of Play

Interlude 6

Weekend Warriors Epilogue

CHRIS. Soooo, "an honest day's work" isn't twenty hours now. And weekends exist.

TAYLOR. Fewer orphans get squashed by machinery. So that's a plus.

CHRIS. Did you notice how there was trying and getting rejected a bunch of times before anything changed though?

MARLEY. Agggh I guess . . . But . . . but . . . urgh. What if I can't do it? What if I try and keep procrastinating anyway?

TAYLOR. Considering that last time, you invented time travel, worst case scenario you'll break the sound barrier or something.

Switcheroo Prologue

MARLEY. I wouldn't procrastinate at all if I lived before the internet.

TAYLOR. I suspect you would find a way.

CHRIS. I'm with Marley on this one. I wouldn't even know most of the news without the internet. I would probably be so calm.

TAYLOR. The news would still happen, you just wouldn't know.

MARLEY. Somebody posts a picture of their dog, you're supposed to not tell them what a great dog it is? What are you, a monster?

TAYLOR. You would rather not see any pictures of dogs at all?

CHRIS. I'm just saying, it was simpler. Less information, it's easier to mind your own business and focus.

TAYLOR. If you think before the internet everybody minded their own business, you have clearly never met my grandma.

MARLEY. No, I met her one time. We're Facebook friends. She comments on literally all my posts.

TAYLOR. That's not the point! You can't just blame the internet.

CHRIS. So let's go back to when it's only telephones and find out if that's a simpler time.

TAYLOR. Okay, fine. But after that can we please go to the future?

MARLEY. You're like a little kid going "are we there yet?" We are going to the 1940s and that's final!

TAYLOR. Please please pleeeease.

    (Time jump!)

SWITCHEROO
by Mora V. Harris

Cast of Characters

MABEL, a romantic young switchboard operator. Good at her job when she feels like it. Easily distracted.

GILDA, a wry young switchboard operator. Loves the rulebook and saving the day. Easily annoyed.

Offstage Voices

SCOTT, a vocally blessed young man, sounds like a total catch.

BROMWELL, speaks with a cool and clipped British accent, sounds like a mastermind.

HOFF, a gruff and gravelly fella, his voice has seen things.

Setting

1940.

Production Notes

This play moves fast! The switchboard operators barely have to pause between answering the call and making the connection, they know their boards so well.

/s indicate places where a line is overlapped by the line that follows (or the buzzing of the switchboard).

Offstage voices may be performed live or recorded.

SWITCHEROO
by Mora V. Harris

(1940. The switchboard office in the basement of the Princess Hotel. Seated in swivel chairs with wheels, GILDA and MABEL are busily answering calls and connecting them on their switchboards.)

GILDA. Princess Hotel. How may I direct your call? / Thank you.

(Buzz! MABEL answers. GILDA connects her caller.)

MABEL. Princess Hotel. / How may I direct your call? Thank you.

(Buzz! GILDA answers. MABEL connects her caller.)

GILDA. Princess Hotel. How may I direct your call? Thank you.

(GILDA connects her caller. Double Buzz! Both answer.)

GILDA and MABEL. *(Unison:)* Princess Hotel. How may I direct your call? Thank you.

(They connect their callers.)

(They wait for a moment to see if either switchboard will buzz.)

MABEL. So anyway, last night—

(Buzz!!! GILDA answers.)

GILDA. Princess Hotel. How may I direct your call? Thank you.

(She connects them.)

You were saying—

(Buzz! MABEL answers.)

GILDA. Oh for the love of Pete.

MABEL. Princess Hotel. How may I direct your call? Oh and who might I say is calling?

(She giggles. GILDA glares disapprovingly.)

MABEL. I'll transfer you straight away. Oh, it's my pleasure.

(Buzz! GILDA answers, absently.)

GILDA. Princess Hotel—

MABEL. I'm sorry, who did you say you wanted?

(GILDA is distracted by MABEL's continuing to go off-script.)

GILDA. How may I . . . Thank you.

81

(GILDA *connects the call.*)

(MABEL *giggles again.*)

MABEL. Right. Mr. Bolton. Bromwell. One moment. Thank you.

GILDA. What was that all about?

MABEL. I'm in love!

GILDA. You weren't using the approved script. And you giggled. A lot.

MABEL. Gilda, you should have heard this voice! It was the voice of a demigod.

GILDA. Just a demi? I'll pass.

MABEL. It was like the sound of chocolate melting.

(MABEL's *switchboard buzzes.*)

MABEL. The sound of silk draping around a diamond in a Cartier ad.

(*Buzz!*)

The sound of my heart dropping into my stomach and exploding into a million butterflies.

(*Buzz!* GILDA *wheels over to* MABEL's *switchboard and answers the call.* MABEL *dreamily twirls in her chair.*)

GILDA. Princess Hotel. How may I direct your call? Thank you.

MABEL. I bet he's handsome. I bet he looks like Lawrence Olivier!

GILDA. Who?

MABEL. Mr. Scott!

(*Buzz!*)

GILDA. Princess Hotel. How may I direct your call? My apologies for the inconvenience, Mr. Scott, I'll reconnect you.

MABEL. Is that him?

GILDA. You sent him to the wrong room!

(MABEL *wrestles* GILDA *for her headset.*)

MABEL. Yes, hello. Calling Mr. Bromwell again? Oh yes, it's me, the first girl. MABEL!

(MABEL *throws a hand over mouth, surprised by her own volume.*)

Yes, I'll connect you.

(MABEL *connects the call and then presses down on the listening key to hear Mr. Scott's conversation.*)

SCOTT. Hey, Marty, sorry about before. Listen are you free for dinner this evening? I'd like to talk over a few things with you before the meeting tomorrow.

GILDA. Mabel, hang up!

MABEL. Shh!

BROMWELL. Yes, I should be available. Why don't you meet me in the hotel lobby about six o'clock? We'll grab a bite.

SCOTT. That's excellent. Hey, and bring Sheila if you'd like.

MABEL. Sheila?

(MABEL *throws a hand over her mouth.* GILDA *tries to press* MABEL's *listening key off and* MABEL *swats her away.*)

SCOTT. What's that?

BROMWELL. Oh Scotty, I'm quite sure my wife would rather listen to her radio program than talk business with the two of us.

SCOTT. I don't blame her. See you at six?

BROMWELL. Until then.

(*The men hang up.*)

GILDA. You're going to get in trouble for that one of these days!

MABEL. Oh, you won't tell on me— You haven't yet. Anyway, it was worth it for that call.

GILDA. I know I'm going to regret asking this, but why?

MABEL. He was inviting his friend Mr. Bromwell to dinner.

GILDA. Sounds pretty mundane to me.

MABEL. Mundane? Mundane? HE'S SINGLE!

GILDA. How do you know that?

MABEL. Because Scotty said—

GILDA. — Scotty?

MABEL. Mr. Bromwell called him Scotty.

GILDA. So his full name is Scotty Scott?

MABEL. Well we don't know what his middle name is yet. It could be something gorgeous. Like Francisco! Or Alphonse!

GILDA. Well, it couldn't be Scott right? Because that would be ridiculous.

MABEL. His name is not Scotty Scott Scott! ANYWAY, when Scotty said Mr. Bromwell should bring Sheila, Mr. Bromwell didn't say, "Oh you should bring Marianne," that's just proper etiquette and Mr. Bromwell sounds British and fancy, so he would have invited Marianne if Marianne existed but she doesn't! So stands to reason—Single.

GILDA. I bet you were top of your class.

MABEL. Unless you think they're both traveling from out of town and for some reason Scotty's wife couldn't come—

GILDA. What if this fella looks like a horse?

(Buzz! GILDA answers.)

/ Princess Hotel. How may I direct your call? Thank you

MABEL. / Ahem, does he SOUND like he looks like horse?

GILDA. What would that sound like?

MABEL. I need to touch up my lipstick in case he calls again. You'll watch my board won't you?

GILDA. Do I have a choice?

MABEL. Thanks doll!

(MABEL exits.)

(GILDA's board buzzes and she answers.)

GILDA. Princess Hotel. How may I direct your call?

HOFF. Yeah, get me Jeff Bromwell.

GILDA. Oh, is this . . . Mr. Scott?

HOFF. Huh?

GILDA. Huh?

HOFF. What do you know about Mr. Scott?

GILDA. Nothing at all. One moment, I'll connect you.

(GILDA connects the call, then hesitates before pressing the listening key.)

HOFF. Are the pieces in place?

BROMWELL. You'll never believe it but he called me.

HOFF. *(Laughing sinisterly:)* The chump's not gonna know what hit him.

BROMWELL. Everything's set on your end?

HOFF. I'll just be waiting for your signal.

BROMWELL. Six o'clock.

HOFF. Then it's lights out for Scotty Scott Scott.

> *(They both laugh sinisterly for a beat too long. Then the call abruptly cuts out.)*
>
> *(GILDA stares dumbly ahead of her. The switchboard buzzes with numerous calls.)*
>
> *(MABEL re-enters.)*

MABEL. Gilda, you're supposed to be covering me!

> *(She picks up her headset.)*

Princess Hotel. How may I direct your call?

GILDA. I think somebody's going to murder Mr. Scott.

MABEL. *(Into phone:)* Thank you.

> *(She connects the call. To GILDA:)*

WHAT?

GILDA. There was a caller and he seemed strange so I listened in, because I thought "Mabel's always listening in, and I deserve to have a good time," and then he was talking to Mr. Bromwell and he said "Lights out for Scotty Scott Scott." And then they had this creepy laugh fest for longer than was comfortable and then they just hung up! Who just hangs up without saying anything? Sociopaths, that's who! He's done for!

MABEL. They said his full name was Scotty Scott Scott?

GILDA. Mabel focus! We've got to do something!

MABEL. You're right, you're right. Perhaps I'm in shock. I'm not ready to lose him. I was just getting to know him.

GILDA. It's almost six o'clock. That hitman's on his way over to hit him with he doesn't know what!

MABEL. Should we call the police?

GILDA. There isn't time for that. We've got to call Mr. Scott and warn him.

MABEL. Call him? Like on the telephone?

GILDA. *(Sarcastically:)* No, just take the elevator up and yell.

MABEL. No need to get testy.

GILDA. He's in 14B. I'll connect you.

MABEL. Wait, Gilda, I can't call him!

GILDA. Why not?

MABEL. Well . . . Isn't that a bit forward?

GILDA. His life hangs in the balance!

MABEL. I've never called a guy.

GILDA. Mabel, you're an operator.

MABEL. That's different, I just answer!

GILDA. Oh for the love of Pete.

> *(She dials Mr. Scott. The phone rings and rings.)*
>
> *(He's not answering.)*

MABEL. It's five till six. What if he already went down to the lobby. He's seems like a very punctual young man.

GILDA. Darn it, he did sound punctual. Let's go.

> *(They both run out.)*
>
> *(A moment.)*
>
> *(Then, we hear people singing "Happy Birthday" in the lobby upstairs.)*
>
> *(MABEL and GILDA re-enter, downtrodden.)*
>
> *(The phone lines continue to buzz with calls through the following.)*

GILDA. Well, that was a very nice celebration.

MABEL. Yes, for a very . . . neat-looking man.

GILDA. He was neat!

MABEL. Yes, very neat. Neat.

. . .
UGH I'll never love again!

GILDA. Well, I don't know about that, but I sure as heck am not listening in on any calls anymore.

MABEL. Me neither! The worst part is he wasn't even single!

GILDA. The worst part is no one even tried to take him out with a rusty pipe.

MABEL. And he thinks he can get away with not looking like Lawrence Olivier? How dare he not look like Lawrence Olivier? Who does he think he is?

GILDA. "Lights out" must've been referring to turning down the lights for the birthday candles. What a drag.

MABEL. I was worried sick about an averagely neat-looking guy, with an averagely neat-looking wife and a below-average name.

GILDA. Scotty Scott Scott. Who'd kill him?

MABEL. I certainly wouldn't bother.

GILDA. Can you imagine the headlines? "SCOTTY SCOTT SCOTT MURDERER CAUGHTY CAUGHT CAUGHT"
. . .

MABEL. . . . Well, I suppose we had better answer these calls.

GILDA. And remember, we're just connecting them and leaving it at that. No listening, no falling in love, no dot connecting . . .

MABEL. Right. Who are we to infringe on guests' privacy?

GILDA. I for one certainly have better things to do than listen in on private conversations.

(GILDA *and* MABEL *each reconnect to their switchboards.*)

GILDA and MABEL. Princess Hotel. How may I direct your call? Thank you.

(GILDA *glances at* MABEL *and quickly turns away.*)

(MABEL *eyes* GILDA, *then stares at her switchboard.*)

(*A beat and then both women surreptitiously reach to press their listening keys.*)

(*Our ears fill with the sounds of telephone chatter.*)

End of Play

Interlude 7

Switcheroo Epilogue

CHRIS. You know, if the Greatest Generation was creeping on people so hard, I actually feel a little better about ours.

MARLEY. I feel like I'm part of a real legacy of busybodies.

TAYLOR. My grandma. I'm telling you.

CHRIS. I feel like I should apologize to the internet.

A Forest Was This Prologue

MARLEY. I don't know, guys. Maybe in a way I was traveling through time . . . to find my way back home. Maybe I was chasing a way to escape myself, but what I found was my true self. Maybe home—

TAYLOR. Okay, are we done here?

MARLEY. Yeah, let's wrap this up and head back to the present.

TAYLOR. What? Already? No way! Come on!

CHRIS. I thought that's what you wanted! You've been complaining about literally every era in history.

MARLEY. Wait, I just had an epiphany that I need to let go and take a risk. So . . .

(She starts just pressing random buttons.)

CHRIS. Wait, are you just pressing random buttons?

MARLEY. I learned a valuable lesson!

TAYLOR. Is this supposed to be making that noise?

MARLEY. Oh weird, I don't know.

CHRIS. Where are we going? ·

MARLEY. *(Initiating the time jump:)* I don't know!

ALL Aaaaaaaaah!

(Time jump!)

A FOREST WAS THIS
by Patrick Greene

Cast of Characters

JUDY

DAD

MOM

TEDDY

MAN IN THE JUMPSUIT

Setting

A forest-ish.

Production Notes

Everything in the forest can be suggested. In fact, you could do this on a completely bare stage. The actors can bring the setting to life.

But hey, if you want to bring in real trees and grass, go for it.

A FOREST WAS THIS
by Patrick Greene

(A forest. Serene. Idyllic. There is a perfectly built campfire. The trees are impossibly green.)

(Near the fire, holding out her hands to warm them is JUDY, 16, who wears perfect pastel clothing. She takes a deep breath.)

JUDY. Ahhh . . . Beautiful . . . Just beautiful.

(DAD, 40s, enters from SR. He's also in perfect pastel clothing with a sweater tied around his neck.)

DAD. Judy, there you are. Enjoying the fire I see.

JUDY. Enjoying it all, Dad—the fire, the fresh air, the trees, the stars . . . *(Another deep breath.)* Ahhh . . . Just heaven.

(DAD gives JUDY a slightly admonishing look.)

JUDY. I mean . . . *(Another deep breath.)* Ahhh . . . Just non-denominational fantasy of a post-life paradise.

DAD. That's my girl.

JUDY. Where are Mom and Teddy?

DAD. Oh, Teddy, that scamp, he went wandering. Mother is out looking for him. But not to worry. He can't have gotten far.

JUDY. I sure hope he's found a better mood out there.

DAD. Now Judy, Teddy is just at that age where young people begin to question the world around them. It's perfectly natural. You went through that phase yourself, young lady.

JUDY. Not like Teddy.

DAD. No, I guess you're right. Teddy's a bit . . . Well, he's . . . Well, let's remember, there's always the Re-Education Protocol.

(DAD and JUDY laugh . . . for far too long. And then they abruptly stop. Silence. Awkward silence.)

(Noises from off. Approaching.)

DAD. Well, well, speak of the non-denominational horned beast from a fiery fantasy realm . . . Teddy, you scamp.

(TEDDY, 13, walks on from SL. He's in pastels as well, but they are wrinkled and dirty. TEDDY rolls his eyes and sits on the ground, hands in his pockets.)

(MOM, 40s, enters a few paces behind TEDDY. She has perfect hair, perfect pastel clothes, perfect fanny pack, perfectly annoyed expression on her face. She quickly corrects to a perfect, toothy smile.)

MOM. Now then, the family is all together.

TEDDY. *(Under his breath:)* Altogether crazy.

(MOM *shoots* TEDDY *a look. He stares at the ground.*)

DAD. How about a song?

MOM. That's a good idea, Father.

DAD. Let's all gather around this perfect fire.

JUDY. We don't want to get too close though, right, Dad? Because fires burn don't they?

DAD. That they do, Judy. That they do.

JUDY. I want to touch it.

MOM. Judy, that's close enough.

(JUDY *steps closer to the fire.*)

JUDY. The flames call to me.

MOM. Judy . . .

JUDY. What's that Mr. Flame? You want me to hold you?

DAD. Now, Judy we talked about this . . .

JUDY. I want to feel the warm hug of eternity.

(JUDY *lunges towards the fire.* DAD *and* MOM *both grab her and hold her back. Eventually,* JUDY *composes herself, but by then* TEDDY *is laughing.* MOM *gives him a scolding look and he eventually stops.*)

DAD. Now, how about that song?

JUDY. Ooooh, I've got one.

MOM. Then get us started, dear.

JUDY. *(Singing:)* So refreshing. So cool.

DAD. *(Singing:)* You'll drink it, 'cause that's the rule.

MOM. *(Singing:)* It's not a soda. It's not from fruit.

JUDY. *(Singing, really getting into it:)* It's Google Water Substitute.

DAD / MOM / JUDY. *(Harmonizing:)* Google Water Substitute / To hydrate / Google Water Substitute / It's so great / Google Water

Substitute / Some blindness / Google Water Substitute / Don't sue us / Google Water Substitute.

JUDY. *(Singing, really putting her heart into it:)* Goooooogggglllleeee Waaaaaaaaatttttteeeerrrrrr Suuuuuubbbbstiiiiiittttuuuuuutttttteeeee! Yay!

> (MOM *and* DAD *clap.* TEDDY *does not. After the clapping finally dies down,* DAD *looks over at* TEDDY.)

DAD. Teddy, why so glum?

TEDDY. I don't see why we have to be here. I don't see why we just couldn't have stayed home with my books, my beautiful books.

MOM. I'm beginning to think those books of yours are becoming a problem.

TEDDY. I'm beginning to think your face is becoming a problem . . . Sorry. I realized now I crossed a line there.

DAD. It's all part of the phase, son.

JUDY. Books burn. They make Mr. Flame.

TEDDY. What did you say?

JUDY. Nothing. I'm hungry.

MOM. It's not quite time for dinner yet, dear.

JUDY. What shall we do then?

DAD. How about a game?

JUDY. I do love games!

MOM. What shall we play?

TEDDY. How about the going home game where we leave this awful place and go home?

MOM. Oh, Tedward, for once can't you just enjoy yourself.

TEDDY. What's to enjoy?

DAD. Look around you, son. It's beautiful.

JUDY. Yeah, Teddy, just look at the stars up there . . . burning bright . . . **giant fiery balls of flame.** *(Looking up at the night sky:)* What's that Mr. Star? You burn for me? And you . . . you want me to burn for you?

DAD. Judy.

JUDY. Just admiring the stars, Dad.

DAD. They are quite magical.

MOM. What's that constellation up there, dear?

DAD. Which one?

(MOM *points up to the sky.*)

DAD. I believe that's the constellation Bon Jovi.

MOM. That's right . . . Bon Jovi. And over there, that's Nicki Minaj.

JUDY. *(Pointing up)* Look, the Big Diplo.

MOM. It's all just so beautiful.

TEDDY. Are you all crazy? I'm asking seriously.

DAD. Crazy in love with nature, son.

TEDDY. But it's not real.

DAD. But in a way, it is, son.

TEDDY. No. It isn't.

MOM. How about that game?

JUDY. Can I pick?

DAD. Now, Judy, you picked the song. I think it's your brother's turn to choose. What do you say, scamp?

TEDDY. You want me to pick a game? Okay. Fine. I've got a game. It's called Truth or Dare.

DAD. I'm not sure that's the type of game—

TEDDY. You said I could pick! Was that a lie? Are you calling my dad a liar?

DAD. Am I calling me . . . I don't . . . I . . .

TEDDY. Good. Then it's agreed. Truth or Dare. Judy, you're first. So what is it?

JUDY. Okay. I pick dare. Dare me to burn something.

TEDDY. You don't get to pick the dare . . . You just . . . Just listen, okay? Now, dare. Fine. Um . . . I dare you climb that tree.

JUDY. Piece of artificially-sweetened-confection-that-is-only-approved-for-consumption-on-the-anniversary-of-one's-birth. I'll go and burn that tree.

TEDDY. I said climb. You know I said climb.

JUDY. Fine. I'll climb it.

MOM. Okay, that's enough. We're not playing this game. No one is climbing anything.

TEDDY. Why not, Mom?

MOM. How about another song?

TEDDY. Nobody wants to hear another damn jingle.

MOM. Language, Teddy.

JUDY. I want to burn the tree, Dad. I mean climb the tree, Dad.

DAD. I . . . well, my dear . . . the thing is . . . your mother is the one who is really in charge; I'm just kind of . . . more like a figurehead. Being a Dad is mostly ceremonial. So what do you say, Mother?

TEDDY. Yeah, Mom, are we allowed to have any fun.

(TEDDY, JUDY *and* DAD *all await* MOM's *response.*)

MOM. Fine. Climb the tree. Go ahead.

(JUDY *jumps for joy and heads over to the closest tree. She looks up. She puts her arms around the tree. She tries to climb the tree. She doesn't get very far.*)

JUDY. I . . . can't . . . do it.

TEDDY. Why not?

JUDY. It's all slippery. Like climbing a pole.

TEDDY. Ah hah. You hear that? Slippery. Whoever heard of a slippery tree?

DAD. I'm no treeologist . . . (*He thinks on it . . . yeah, that's the word.*) I'm no treeologist, but I believe that yes, trees can be slippery.

TEDDY. You don't need to be a treeologist . . . (*He thinks on it.*) That's not a real word.

DAD. Oh, it is.

TEDDY. Whatever. You don't need to be a tree expert to know a trunk can't be like a slippery pole.

MOM. Judy, that's enough. Get away from that tree.

TEDDY. It's not a tree. It's a pole. It's all fake. All of it. There's no fire. There are no stars. No Bon Jovi constellation. It's fake!

DAD. Your phase is acting up, son.

MOM. Let's eat. I think it's dinner time.

(JUDY *comes back over by the fire.*)

JUDY. But I didn't get a turn. In the game.

MOM. The game is over.

JUDY. But Dad, that's not fair.

DAD. Figurehead, dear.

TEDDY. Just let her have a turn and then we'll eat whatever tasteless mush you packed for us.

MOM. One turn and then the game is over.

JUDY. Yippee. Thank you, Mother. Teddy.

TEDDY. Yeah.

JUDY. Truth or Dare.

TEDDY. Truth. Because truth is the most important thing we have. In a world that is devoid of nature, all we have is—

JUDY. Truth . . . When you look up, what do you see?

TEDDY. Oh come on, really? You could ask me anything and that's all you think to ask?

JUDY. Answer.

TEDDY. Fine.

(TEDDY *looks up.*)

JUDY. Well?

TEDDY. I see lights.

JUDY. What kinds of lights?

TEDDY. Lights that are a part of a holographic scene.

JUDY. What do they look like?

TEDDY. They are meant to look like stars.

JUDY. Could they be real stars?

TEDDY. No.

JUDY. How do you know?

TEDDY. Because I just know. I know this is fake. All of it is fake. We're in a simulation of nature because we live in a world where—

JUDY. I ask again, how do you know?

TEDDY. I'm not an idiot. I just know. I read.

JUDY. You know that what you see is not real because you read it in a book? How do you know that what you read in the book is real? Maybe that's fake.

TEDDY. Oh, come on Judy. We all know this is fake . . . well, maybe not Dad.

DAD. Thanks, son.

JUDY. But they could be. Admit it. You don't know for absolute certain that the stars you see above are not real stars.

TEDDY. Well . . . I know they're fake.

JUDY. But there is a chance they are real. Even a slight chance.

TEDDY. There is an infinitesimal chance that they are actually up there and they are real and that everything I've ever known is wrong.

JUDY. So they could be up there, burning away . . . all that heat . . . the flames . . . the hot, hot, hot flames . . .

TEDDY. Fine, Judy, you're right.

> (TEDDY *looks up again at the stars. He has his hands in his pockets.*)

TEDDY. Maybe, just maybe those are real stars up there.

> (TEDDY *takes a coin from his pocket.*)

TEDDY. But more likely, it's all a hoax.

MOM. What do you have in your hand?

> (TEDDY *holds out a penny.*)

TEDDY. My lucky coin . . . that Grandma gave me.

MOM. We know no Grandma.

DAD. We know no Grandma.

JUDY. We know no Grandma.

TEDDY. Well I do. It's from the year she was born . . . 2008.

> (TEDDY *once again looks up at the stars. He rears back and throws the penny at the sky. It hits something metal. The lights change. Everything goes black. After a moment, the lights go back on but there are no trees. No fire. No stars. Nothing.*)

JUDY. What happened? Where's the fire? My precious flames.

MOM. Teddy!

TEDDY. Well, looky-here. No stars. No trees.

DAD. This is a bad phase, Teddy. Really bad phase.

MOM. (*Looking more afraid than angry:*) Teddy, this is . . . you've gone too far this time.

TEDDY. Can we go home now?

(A MAN IN THE JUMPSUIT *enters from SR. He is holding a tablet. He surveys the scene, only glancing at the family, who are all watching him. After a moment, he stops in front of* TEDDY.*)*

MAN IN THE JUMPSUIT. Okay, you'll be coming with me.

TEDDY. What?

MAN IN THE JUMPSUIT. You're Coin Boy, right?

TEDDY. Coin Boy?

MAN IN THE JUMPSUIT. You're the one who threw the coin and broke the simulation.

TEDDY. Ummm . . . Yeah.

MAN IN THE JUMPSUIT. Then you're coming with me.

MOM. Not so fast. You can't just take my son.

MAN IN THE JUMPSUIT. *(Holding out the tablet to* MOM:*)* Is that your signature?

MOM. Yes.

MAN IN THE JUMPSUIT. Is this boy a member of your party?

MOM. Well . . . yes.

MAN IN THE JUMPSUIT. You signed a document that states, should any member of the attending party intentionally damage the simulation, they will be immediately removed and taken for Re-Education Protocol Number 36.

MOM. Number 36?

TEDDY. Which one is 36 again?

JUDY. Grandma.

DAD. We know no Grandma.

TEDDY. Oh, no, no, no. You can't do that.

MAN IN THE JUMPSUIT. Sorry, kid. She signed the document. It's protocol.

TEDDY. Mom?

*(*MOM *goes over to* TEDDY. *She embraces him.)*

MOM. Mom is more of a . . . ceremonial role. I'm basically a figure-head.

(The MAN IN THE JUMPSUIT *comes over and separates* TEDDY *from* MOM. *He begins to lead* TEDDY *off SR.)*

TEDDY. Mom! Dad!

DAD. At least your phase will be over, son.

TEDDY. But it was just a coin . . . my lucky coin.

(MOM *and* DAD *turn away.*)

TEDDY. Judy!

JUDY. Goodbye, Teddy. If it's any comfort, I'm going to burn your books.

TEDDY. Why would that be comforting to me!!!???

JUDY. It's comforting to me, so . . .

TEDDY. You know what; I'd take Re-Education Protocol Number 36 over this family any day.

DAD. That's a good attitude, son.

(*The* MAN IN THE JUMPSUIT *and* TEDDY *are almost off SR.*)

JUDY. Bye, Teddy.

MAN IN THE JUMPSUIT. You know no Teddy now.

JUDY / MOM / DAD. We know no Teddy.

(*The* MAN IN THE JUMPSUIT *and* TEDDY *exit.*)

JUDY. I'm sad.

DAD. Could be a phase.

MOM. You're probably just hungry, dear.

JUDY. I am hungry, Mom. You're right!

(JUDY *hugs* MOM. *After a moment,* DAD *awkwardly joins the hug. They remain in this embrace until the blackout.*)

JUDY. Mom, why do all of our vacations end with one of my siblings being taken away for some Re-Education Protocol?

MOM. We know no other siblings, honey.

JUDY. Oh, right . . . Hey, Dad?

DAD. Yes, dear.

JUDY. Can we have Italian-inspired-cheesie-dough-wheel for dinner tonight?

DAD. I'm more of a figurehead, dear. Ask you mother.

MOM. You know we can only afford to eat that on non-denomina-tional-winter-gift-certificate-exchange-celebration-eve.

JUDY. Oh . . . right?

MOM. Well, maybe we can make an exception this once.

JUDY. Really?

MOM. Sure.

JUDY. Thanks, Mom.

DAD. See, my darling, isn't life great.

JUDY. Yes. It is. It is. It really is. It is. Yes, it is.

    (Blackout.)

End of Play

Interlude 8

A Forest Was This Epilogue

MARLEY. Well, yikes. Right?

CHRIS. Okay, I feel a little validated for being worried.

MARLEY. It's not a sure thing. According to the Wikipedia page about time travel, it's just one possible future timeline.

CHRIS. So maybe there's still time? How are you doing over there, Taylor? This is literally the quietest you have ever been.

TAYLOR. How am I DOING?!?!? I'm having an existential crisis is how I'm doing!

CHRIS. *(Quoting herself back to her:)* Welcome to being aware of things, my friend.

MARLEY. Maybe you should learn to take a risk like I did about fifteen minutes ago.

TAYLOR. But if there's no easy answers in the past AND no easy answers in the future then what do we have to do? Live in the moment? That's so dumb!

Kids Today! Prologue

CHRIS. I don't know. Maybe it's just hard to be a person, period.

MARLEY. Hey guys—

TAYLOR. What if there's no time in all of history when everything is clear?

CHRIS. *(Panicking:)* We just go ON like this?

TAYLOR. The blind leading the blind?

MARLEY. GUYS?!?! The time machine—

CHRIS. Lost forever in the great struggle that is humanity!

MARLEY. GUYS!!! The time machine! Something—

TAYLOR. — Marley, we're kind of having a moment here!

MARLEY. It's malfunctioning! The time machine is malfunctioning!

TAYLOR. Should we press a bunch more buttons again?

MARLEY & CHRIS. NOOOOOOOOO!

ALL. AAAAAAAAAAAAAAHHHHHHH!!!!!!!!!!

(Time jump, but it's a little different than the other ones somehow!)

101

KIDS TODAY!
by Ian McWethy

Cast of Characters

CHILD
PARENT

Setting

2015 . . . at first

Production Notes

Hello! And thank you for doing my play *Kids Today!*. A couple of thoughts on the casting, because there are a few different ways you could do it.

1. With two actors. With the Child and Parent switching roles each scene (or time jump). This is how the play is written.

2. There's an equally interesting version if you want to cast five actors. In this version, a new actor is cast every time you jump back 30 years. So the Parent in 2015 will still become the Child in 1985, but then a different actor will play Parent 1985.

Gosh this could get confusing. (Time travel! Why are you always so complicated!)

Here's a casting breakdown if you perform this with five actors.

ACTOR A: CHILD 2015, PARENT 2035
ACTOR B: PARENT 2015, CHILD 1985
ACTOR C: PARENT 1985, CHILD 1955
ACTOR D: PARENT 1955
ACTOR E: CHILD 2035

Does that (sort of) make sense?

The only other thing you'd need to change is in the "time dispersement scene" in the 1955 sequence. My thought would be that ALL the actors could come onstage during that section, each taking different lines, creating a sort of "ensemble time montage" thing. I don't know how you stage that but . . . it could be cool!

Other than that . . . have fun. If you want to change the specific references or make little line changes here or there you can. But if you want to make drastic changes please email Playscripts or me first. This play could unravel if you start to make big changes.

Good luck!
Ian.McWethy@gmail.com

KIDS TODAY!
by Ian McWethy

(2015)

(CHILD, 16, sits on the floor, cross-legged. They are engrossed in their phone, watching game plays on Twitch.)

(A PARENT comes on stage and puts a backpack on the floor. PARENT looks in the bag, double-checking the gear so that they can go on a hike.)

PARENT. Okay. I've got Clif bars. An extra phone charger. Water. Sun tan lotion SPF 65. And we are ready to hike! You ready to . . . uh, what are you doing?

CHILD. What?

PARENT. What do you mean what? Why are you just sitting there!? I said be ready in 10 minutes. That was 20 minutes ago!

CHILD. Oh my god! Who cares. It's not like it's gonna matter if we're late to a hike! The trail isn't going to get up and leave! The world won't suddenly end!

PARENT. Well what are you doing that's so important! Are you texting Rachel. Ooooo—

CHILD. Dad. Stop. Rachel hasn't even been in school this year, she has mono!

PARENT. Well show me! Come on, show me!

(PARENT tries to take the phone out of CHILD's hand. CHILD resists. Moves away. Always looking at the phone.)

CHILD. Stop! Can you just stop.

PARENT. Come on! I just want to get what you're doing. Come on. Come on, come on, come on, come on—

CHILD. *(Snapping:)* Uh! Fine. You're so annoying. I'm just blitzin' a game play on 1.5 speed. See?

PARENT. You're blitzing a . . . sorry, you're what?

CHILD. I'm watching. A. Game. Play. On Twitch. See.

(CHILD show PARENT the phone. PARENT looks at it.)

PARENT. Oh. You're playing a video game. I know video games. I used to be a master at Super Mario World 3 when I was your age.

Not to brag but I was the first one in my neighborhood to find the secret whistle on level—

CHILD. A game!? No. I'm not playing a game! Why would I play a game?!

PARENT. Because it's . . . fun?

CHILD. Twitch is a streaming service with over 20,000 channels where you watch partners play games and comment on livestreams. Bug-BugX9 is my favorite. He's hella funny. But also he's like really progressive, because unlike PewDiePie he doesn't—

PARENT. No, no, no. Stop. Hold on. You're . . . saying you are just watching somebody else . . . play a video game.

CHILD. Yeah.

PARENT. And you don't play them yourself. You just . . . watch someone else . . . play it.

CHILD. Yeah.

(PARENT *paces around the room. Furious.*)

PARENT. I'm sorry, but you can't . . . I won't allow you to do this anymore.

CHILD. What do you mean I'm not allowed to do this! What's your problem?

PARENT. Video games are one thing! I played video games! With my friends! It taught me problem solving and developed my hand-eye coordination! But we didn't just sit and watch! The only person who sat and watched was Benny Belson and he was a weird, little antisocial loser who would eat his own scabs! And my son will not be a scab eater!

CHILD. Dad! This isn't antisocial! I'm regularly talking to like 15 people all over the world while I watch!

PARENT. Well not any more you're not.

(PARENT *stuffs the phone in their pocket!*)

PARENT. No phone! No internet! Until you learn to socialize like a normal human being!

CHILD. Are you serious right now! God, I— I— You just don't get anything! I hate you!

(The CHILD *stomps offstage.*)

(While PARENT *gives the following mini-monologue, they unbutton their polo shirt. Mess up their hair. Take off their polo shirt revealing a younger t-shirt from the 80s.)*

PARENT. It's for your own good. I know you may not understand now but I promise you . . . it is for your own good. I was young once too, ya know. I was . . . uh . . . I was . . .

(PARENT *takes out a Nintendo controller and sits on the floor, right where* CHILD *was sitting.* PARENT *is now . . .)*

(1985)

(. . . CHILD. *Playing Nintendo. Hyper-focused. Doesn't even look up when* PARENT *enters from stage left.)*

(PARENT *goes to the pack [which was left on the floor].* PARENT *checks the contents to make sure they have everything.)*

PARENT. Okay. I've got PowerBars. Clip-on sunglasses for my actual glasses. Water. Sun tan lotion SPF 15. And we are ready to hike! You ready to . . . uh, what are you doing? Why aren't you ready to go?

CHILD. Oh my God! Who cares. Hikes are boring!

PARENT. Hikes are boring! Hikes are— And what are you doing that's so important that you can't be on time! Come on. Turn off your cartoons and let's—

CHILD. It's not cartoons Mom! It's NES. Chucky let me borrow it while he's on vacation so I really have to maximize my time with it. It's . . . mind-blowing. Super Mario Brothers is maybe the best thing that's ever been invented.

PARENT. Oh. Okay. It's NES. So this is like a . . . VCR for cartoons or—?

CHILD. No! Look at the controller in my hand! This is a video game. Video. Game. Okay? I'm Mario, and the object is to rescue the princess from King Koopa. But if a koopa troopa, a goomba, or Boos touch you, you're dead. Especially when you get to castle levels, there are Boos everywhere! It's crazy.

(PARENT *is utterly baffled.)*

PARENT. I don't . . . I don't understand anything you just said.

CHILD. Of course you don't. You're old. You like to go on hikes.

PARENT. Hey! Don't knock hiking. I went on hikes with my parents and one day you'll wanna go on hikes with your kids.

CHILD. Mom. I promise you, I will never, ever want to go on a hike. Even the word hike makes me wanna barf. Hike! Uh!

PARENT. Well listen, you're not gonna sit inside and rot your brains playing this thing. I'm not going to let my daughter *(or son)* end up like Betty Buckman.

CHILD. Who? What are you talking about?

PARENT. Betty Buckman was a strange, creepy girl I grew up with. And while everyone I knew was out having fun, getting milk shakes and going to the movies, she was at the penny arcade. Playing pinball 6–10 hours a day! And if you asked for a turn she would lick your palm. Like a lizard. Like a weird, horny lizard! And no son of mine is going to be a horny lizard like Betty Buckman!

CHILD. What are you talking about?! I don't even care about lizards!

PARENT. Then why are you making that Italian plumber jump on that turtle!?

CHILD. Because that's how you beat the game! And It's not a turtle it's a koopa troopa!

PARENT. That is nonsense! You know what! Go to your room! And don't come out until you stop being weird about lizards!

CHILD. Oh my God! You just don't get anything! God! I hate you!

(CHILD *stomps offstage.*)

(PARENT, *again, unbuttons their polo as they give the following mini-monologue, revealing a t-shirt underneath.* PARENT *sits on the floor, on the same spot* CHILD *was sitting, and takes out a magazine with James Dean on the cover.*)

PARENT. Oh, okay! Fine. You hate me! Fine! Look, you're not as smart as you think! I was young once too! I remember . . . uh . . .

(PARENT *is now . . .*)

(1955)

(. . . CHILD. *Reading the magazine. Hyper focused. Doesn't even look up when* PARENT *enters from stage left.* PARENT *goes to the pack, looks inside.*)

PARENT. Okay. I've got beef jerky. A bug spray not approved by any government regulatory agency, but I'm sure it's safe. Water. And finally a weird, white zinc substance that only goes on my nose. That should definitely protect me from sunburns. And we are ready to hike! You ready to . . . uh, what are you doing?

CHILD. What?

PARENT. What do you mean what? Why are you just sitting there!? I said be ready in 10 minutes.

CHILD. Oh my God! Who cares. Hikes are boring. It's not like it matters if we're—

PARENT. Hikes are boring? Hikes are— And what are you doing that's so important!

CHILD. I'm reading about James Dean. The actor. Maybe the most important actor ever!

PARENT. Oh Geez. You and that movie! You know I went and saw that Rebel movie you're so obsessed with and I have to say . . . I was kind of disturbed by it. And that . . . that Dean actor! He's terrible!

CHILD. Dad! What are you talking about? James Dean is probably the greatest actor I've ever seen. He's so . . . raw and realistic and—

PARENT. But all he does is—is mumble. And shout. And then he cried! Really cried! A grown man!

CHILD. Yeah! That's acting!

PARENT. No! Not it's not! Gary Cooper never cried. John Wayne never cried! The actors I grew up with didn't cry because that's not what actors do!

CHILD. You just don't get it!

PARENT. Look, you're not going to sit in a dark room, watching a movies like . . . Billie Bean. He was weird little introvert who spent his days at the local Vaudeville eating gum off the seats! And no son *(or daughter)* of mine is going to end up like Betty Buckman!

CHILD. Betty Buckman? I thought you said his name was Billie Bean.

PARENT. I didn't say Betty Buckman! I said his name was Bobby Benson. I don't want you . . .

PARENT. Being a little weirdo like Bobby Benson.

CHILD. Being a little weirdo like Bobby Benson.

> *(They look at each other.* CHILD *confused, aware of the time dispersion.* PARENT *not.)*

> *(The lights change slowly. Somehow darker yet more focused on our two main characters.)*

CHILD. Betty. Bobby. Billie . . . haven't we . . . done this before?

PARENT. Done what before? What are you talking about?

CHILD. It's the weirdest thing. I don't how to explain it but I swear we've done this. Or will do this. Or are doing this.

PARENT. Doing what? What are you talking about?

CHILD. Fighting. And hiking! Why do you keep trying to get me to go on a hike?!

PARENT. Because it's what I did with my parents! And I want to share it with you!

CHILD. But you hated it when you were my age! Why would you make me do it if you hated it?!

PARENT. Because it was character building! Look, you'll understand when you're older.

CHILD. I don't think I will.

PARENT. It's hard for you to understand now, but one day you will. This . . . this radio that you're so obsessed with! It's bad for you!

CHILD. I don't think it is.

PARENT. This jazz music! It's bad for you!

CHILD. It's not!

PARENT. The printing press! It's bad for you! It's putting the devil's thoughts in your head and I . . . I need to protect you from it! From all of it!

CHILD. But you can't. There's nothing you can do. There's nothing any of us can do. Time is inevitable so why can't you just . . . stop!

> (PARENT, *now suddenly very honest, hurt, scared, slowly walks backwards off stage.*)

PARENT. You think you can. You think you'll be different. But there are some truths that can't be denied: A parent will always love their child. And that love will terrify that parent. Because it's just so much! **It is ever expanding and overwhelming and defies the laws** of anything that a parent has ever known before. And therefore the only way they know how to respond is . . . is . . . to make their family go on a hike. A hike that no one wants to go on.

CHILD. But why?!

PARENT. Because. It's what we did. And it keeps us moving.

> (*And then the* PARENT *is gone.*)

(The CHILD *digs through the bag and finds an adult shirt. A spotlight focuses on* CHILD *as they hastily puts their shirt on and fix their hair to become* PARENT *as they say the following.)*

CHILD. It can't just be like this! There's no reason this has to keep happening! Change is vital, isn't it?! If we don't change then we're . . . we're stuck! We'll make the same mistakes over and over and over again until we—

OTHER CHILD. *(Offstage:)* Mom! *(Or Dad.)* What are you talking about?!

(The lights come back on the stage. CHILD, *leaning over the hiking bag, is now* PARENT.*)*

(A new CHILD *is sitting on the ground, seemingly playing a virtual game with just their hands.)*

(2035)

PARENT. I was just um . . . I was . . . I was just going over the list of . . . what we need for a hike. Sunglass eye contacts. SPF 200. Iodine water tablets since all the earth's drinking water is now polluted and will make you sick.

CHILD. Oh my God! Mom! I really don't want to go on a hike today! I've got way too much Vrooking to do today. And besides! Hiking is so boring!

PARENT. But we planned this for a week! I told you how important it was. I did it with my parents and they—uh—uh . . .

CHILD. What?

PARENT. Nothing. I . . . sorry I'm just getting a weird feeling. Like I . . .

(After a beat, where PARENT *tries to make sense of a weird feeling:)*

You know what? If you don't want to go on a hike. You don't have to hike. That's okay.

CHILD. It is? Sweet! Awe thanks. I've just been off the V-grid all week and I'm like, super behind on my kills, ya know.

PARENT. Sure. I don't understand but . . . sure. Have fun Vrooking.

*(*PARENT *turns to walk offstage, then stops themselves.)*

PARENT. Actually, um, could I . . . do that? Could I Vrook, with you?

CHILD. You wanna Vrook? On the V-Grid?

PARENT. Sure. If you'd . . . be willing to teach me.

CHILD. Uh. I guess. I don't think you'll like it but . . . sure. So, at first I'll start you on a pretty basic training exercise. You'll need to master it first before uploading you onto the V-Grid. So grab those VR eye contacts over there, and that will upload you to the training program. V-Grid is like . . . it's a completely augmented reality, scientists say it's actually feels more realistic than real life.

> (PARENT *picks up a pair of eye contact lenses and puts them in their eyes.* PARENT *is immediately transported to a hyperreal VR world [but to us, it looks like nothing]. Maybe a sound cue indicates* PARENT *has been uploaded. Like the sound of a MacBook turning on or something.*)

PARENT. Okay, so I just put these in then. . . . OH MY GOD! Whoa! This is . . . very realistic. Wow!

CHILD. Told you. V-Grid is more real than reality. Okay, so once you're trained enough in the VR—Vrooking simulator, you'll be to go out and punch people to death with your bare hands. But that's—

PARENT. You What?! I don't want you murder-punching people, this is way too realistic! It's gonna turn you into Barney Bloomenthal and—

CHILD. Mom! It's not like I'm punching innocent people. They've all been possessed by a vampire lizard named Dean. Okay. And who's Barney? Why would I end up like Barney?

> (PARENT *thinks.*)

PARENT. Nothing. He was just a guy I knew when I was your age. But . . . it doesn't matter. You're, right, you're nothing like him. Sorry, let's keep playing this.

CHILD. Are you sure? You don't have to if you don't want to.

PARENT. No, I'm sure. I— I want to do this. I want to know what it is you do for . . . fun.

> (*A mini beat. Then . . .*)

CHILD. Okay! Siri-Alexa! Start a Vrook session.

> (PARENT *and* CHILD, *together, start walking in place. As if on a treadmill.*)

PARENT. Oh Geez! Okay. Wow. So, what do we do?

CHILD. Just Vrook. Or, you know, walk for now. Before you do any of the fun stuff you really have to get a handle on walking. So . . . we'll just do that for the next hour or so.

(They walk.)

CHILD. So what do you think? It's cool, right?

PARENT. Yeah. It is.

(They continue to walk as the lights slowly fade.)

End of Play

A Simpler Time: Epilogue

ALL. . . . AAAAAAAAAAAAAAAAAAAH!

CHRIS. Am I alive? Are we alive?

MARLEY. We lived! We made it!

TAYLOR. I knew pressing a bunch of buttons at the same time would work out. What just happened?

MARLEY. I think it was some kind of a wormhole! Because, that was a couple of times. At once!

CHRIS. Well, where are we now?

MARLEY. I think . . . hey. It's the present.

> *(Beat, as they consider this.)*

CHRIS. . . . Okay.

TAYLOR. Huh.

MARLEY. How do we feel about that?

CHRIS. I mean . . . sure.

TAYLOR. Yeah. Like, okay.

MARLEY. Right. Me too.

CHRIS. I think . . . I think maybe there is no simpler time to be a person. The circumstances change but people are always kind of ridiculous.

TAYLOR. Huh.

MARLEY. Wow.

> *(Beat.)*

MARLEY. Soooooo . . . the simpler time . . . was inside us all along?

CHRIS. Shut up.

TAYLOR. The simpler time was the friends we made along the way!

CHRIS. Absolutely not.

MARLEY. The simpler time is the time you spend with your best friends in a deceptively low-budget time machine.

CHRIS. EMAIL THE GUY, MARLEY.

MARLEY. I know. I'm gonna! Quit freaking out about the future if you're not going to do anything about it!

CHRIS. OKAY, I learned a valuable lesson! I'm contacting my elected officials!!!! But my bunker days are done.

TAYLOR. Yeah, I'm not going to live in your bunker but I'm not going to assume things are going to just work out. We should mostly be okay, but I want NO PART of that scary possible timeline.

MARLEY. Good because if either of you live in a bunker I'm going to pretend I don't know you.

CHRIS. You know what though, I do think there is still one simpler time we can recapture.

MARLEY. I'm afraid the time machine is pretty much fried.

CHRIS. I'm talking about the era of pizza as the ultimate reward for a job well done.

TAYLOR. YESSS I'm so hungry! I can't believe we didn't get a snack in any century. Can we get a large?

MARLEY. Look guys, we aren't kids anymore. We broke the space-time continuum. So, I think we also earned garlic bread.

ALL. Yeah!

End of Play

Author Biographies

Jonathan Dorf has had his plays produced throughout the United States and Canada, as well as on every continent except Antarctica. He has been a finalist for the Actors Theatre of Louisville Heideman Award, the Weinberger Playwright Residency, the Charlotte Repertory New Play Festival, and the InterAct New Play Festival. His work has been seen at Playwrights Theatre of New Jersey, Ensemble Studio Theatre - LA, Moving Arts, and the Pittsburgh New Works Festival, and he has had plays for young people commissioned by the Walnut Street Theatre, Coachella Valley Repertory, and the Choate Rosemary Hall Summer Arts Conservatory, where he served as playwright-in-residence. In addition to his many works with Playscripts, plays include *Ben, Bookends, Shining Sea, Milk and Cookies, Beef Junkies, Supermodels in Jeopardy,* and *Neverland,* while such works as *4 A.M. (the musical), From Shakespeare With Love?, Now You See Me, Dear Chuck, War of the Buttons,* and *Me, My Selfie & I* were created specifically for school-age actors and audiences. A number of his monologues are published in collections by Playscripts, Inc., Meriwether and Smith & Kraus, and his published plays make their homes at Playscripts, Inc., Brooklyn Publishers, Heuer, Original Works, and YouthPLAYS, the publisher of plays for young actors and audiences he co-founded. He is also co-created ProduceaPlay.com, the web's foremost resource site for producers, and authored Young Playwrights 101, a complete playwriting text for young playwrights and those who teach them.

Long-time playwriting advisor for Final Draft and The Writers Store (author of Playwriting101.com and playwriting instructor at Screenwriters University), Mr. Dorf has also served as Visiting Associate Professor of Theatre in the graduate playwriting and children's literature programs at Hollins University, and as the United States cultural envoy to Barbados. He is the co-chair of the Alliance of Los Angeles Playwrights, a life member and former managing director of the Philadelphia Dramatists Center, and a member of the Dramatists Guild of America and the Guild's education committee. He holds a BA in Dramatic Writing and Literature from Harvard University and an MFA in Playwriting from UCLA, and works with playwrights and screenwriters internationally as a script consultant. He has been a guest artist at the International Thespian Festival, Educational Theatre Association Annual Conference, Asian Festival of Children's Content, the Tennessee Arts Academy, as well as at numerous schools and festivals. He is available for playwriting workshops and residencies worldwide through his JonathanDorf. com website.

Tyler Dwiggins is a New York-based playwright and screenwriter. His first play, **Bump**, has been showcased at Actors Theatre of Louisville, FSU/Asolo Conservatory, and received a nomination for the National Partners - American Theatre Award at the Kennedy Center American College Theatre Festival. His plays for young actors, *subText, Orange Is the New Glass,* and *Unbreakable Timmy Cratchit,* are published by Playscripts. Tyler was a member of the BMI Lehman Engel Musical Theatre Librettists Workshop and the Project Y Playwrights Group. He has been selected as a semifinalist for the Bay Area Playwrights Festival, The Ground Floor at Berkeley Rep, and the Orchard Project Episodic Lab. He has served as a teaching artist at Northwestern University's National High School Institute (Cherubs). Tyler is the writer and creator of the LGBTQ web series, *Queen's English.*

Claire Epstein is a graduate of Vanderbilt University and Circle in the Square Theatre School. She's originally from Washington, DC, and currently lives in Los Angeles. She is the author of fifteen novels (written under a pseudonym), which have sold hundreds of thousands of copies and been translated internationally.

Kathryn Funkhouser. Kathryn's plays *Double Double and Unbreakable Timmy Cratchit* are published by Playscripts. Other plays include *Bootstraps, Help Who's Next, Accessories, Alternative Facts, We're Not So Different, You and I, The Sequel, The Pitch,* and *Ghost Story* (Oxnam Award, EST and Drew University). She produced The Resistance Cabaret at the Tank Theater in NYC in 2017. Her articles and essays have appeared in publications such as The Toast, McSweeney's Internet Tendency, the *Atlantic,* and the *Nation.* BA from Drew University. Memberships: Athena Writes (2018) and the Project Y Playwrights Group. She lives in Brooklyn with a lot of original cast albums. kathrynfunkhouser.com.

Patrick Greene lives in New York City with his wife, but no longer any cats.

Mora V. Harris writes character-driven comedies under a blanket in Pittsburgh, Pennsylvania. Notable productions of her work include The Weird Sisters Theatre Project, The Women's Theatre Festival, 5th Wall Productions, and Pittsburgh Opera, in addition to multiple productions at high schools and colleges. Her work has received development through City Theatre Company, The Hangar Theatre, Alliance/Kendeda, the Sewanee Writers' Conference, and the Kennedy Center's Eugene O'Neill Theatre Center Fellowship. She was a two-time National Finalist for the Kennedy Center's John Cauble Award for Outstanding Short Play, and a Second Place winner of the Alfred P. Sloan Script Competition. She holds a B.A. in Creative Writing and Theater from Oberlin College and an M.F.A. in Dramatic Writing from Carnegie Mellon University where she studied with Rob Handel. She works as a teaching artist for City Theatre and teaches writing at the University of Pittsburgh. www.moravharris.com.

Carrie McWethy (McCrossen). Carrie is an actor/writer/comedian. She's appeared Off-Broadway and on television (*Divorce, The Rundown, Late Night Snack,* and, surprisingly, *Star Talk with Neil DeGrasse Tyson*). But she's best known for appearing in sketch videos that are passed around your Facebook feed (Funny or Die, Above Average, UCB Comedy, College Humor, etc.). Carrie's Playscripts plays include *Don't Blame Me, I'm Just the Playwright,* and *This is Your Brain on Social Media* (with husband Ian McWethy). She's also published both one-act and full-length adaptations of *The Scarlet Letter* for Stage Partners, Inc. Her ten-minute play, *I Do, You Die,* which was originally performed at the Upright Citizens Brigade Theater, is now being presented all over the world.

Carrie is a house performer of both improv and sketch at the Upright Citizens Brigade Theater. Her solo show, *M.I.L.P: Moms I'd Like to Portray* ran at the Upright Citizens Brigade Theater in 2016. Her one-act All in Favor; a Meeting of the Beulah, North Dakota Town Council, ran in 2017. She's written and produced videos for NickMom, iVillage and CH2, and is a regular contributor to FunnyorDie. Carrie co-wrote and starred in *For Maya,* (an indie short) which was an official selection HollyShorts, Nitehawk, High Falls and Brooklyn Comedy Festivals, and a Vimeo staff pick. Carrie's pilot script, *Subscribe Now,* was a finalist for the 2016 Nantucket Film Festival Tony Cox Award, the Made in NY Writer's Room fellowship, and a semi-finalist for the Fox Writers Lab. www.carriemccrossen.com

Ian McWethy's plays include *Moral Values...*, *Actors are Stupid, Bad Auditions by Bad Actors, and 12 Incompetent Jurors.* Thirty of his one-act plays have been published by Playscripts, Inc. and Stage Partners and have been performed in all fifty states as well as internationally in over 30 different countries. He's also written several screenplays, sitcom pilots, short films, and a webseries. He's happily married to Carrie McCrossen and splits his time between California and New York. Mr. McWethy is represented by Bradford Bricken of Cartel Management.

Don Zolidis holds a B.A. in English from Carleton College and an M.F.A. in playwriting from the Actor's Studio Program at the New School University, where he studied under Romulus Linney.

His plays have been seen at numerous theatres around the country, including The Purple Rose Theatre, The Ensemble Studio Theatre, The Bloomington Playwright's Project, The Phoenix Theatre, the Victory Theatre, Stage West, The Williamstown Theatre, and many others.

Don received the Princess Grace Award for playwriting in 2004 after having twice been a finalist. His plays have received two Edgerton New Play awards and multiple NEA grants among other honors. In 2013 his play *White Buffalo* was nominated for the Pulitzer Prize for Drama.

His plays for young people are among the most-produced in the country and have received more than 7,500 productions, appearing in every state and 51 countries.

Also available from **PLAYSCRIPTS**

SCARED SILLY
10 Hauntingly Hilarious Short Plays

by Peter Bloedel, Christa Crewdson,
Hillary DePiano, Jonathan Dorf,
Patrick Greene, Alan Haehnel,
Ian McWethy, Ed Monk,
Becca Schlossberg,
& Don Zolidis

Comedy, 100-120 minutes
8 females, 8 males, 14 either
(16-85 actors possible: 8-62 f, 8-54 m)

We challenged ten playwrights to bring us their funniest takes on the fearsome in this collection of ten-minute plays. Designed to be flexible for your evil plans, these plays can be performed in any combination. Every spooky tale in this collection has a twist, whether it's what detention looks like in a school for the supernatural (*The Midnight Club*), what happens when a slasher-movie junkie tries to track down a killer (*It's You!*), the incredible secret of the trick-or-treater dressed normally who wants candy anyway (*The True Meaning of Halloween*), or the only thing that scares ghosts (*In the Waiting Room at the Ghost Placement Agency*).

- **The Kev-Burger** by Peter Bloedel
- **The Rocky Junction Rumor** by Christa Crewdson
- **The (Completely Inaccurate) Legend of the Mummy Witch House** by Hillary DePiano
- **The Midnight Club** by Jonathan Dorf
- **In the Waiting Room at the Ghost Placement Agency, Life Comes at You Fast** by Patrick Greene
- **Left Hanging** by Alan Haehnel
- **It's You!** by Ian McWethy
- **Attack of the Cafeteria Zombies** by Ed Monk
- **Forever Friends** by Becca Schlossberg
- **The True Meaning of Halloween** by Don Zolidis

Order online at **PLAYSCRIPTS.COM**